Hunting
The American
Wild Turkey

Hunting The American Wild Turkey

by Dave Harbour

Stackpole Books

HUNTING THE AMERICAN WILD TURKEY

Copyright © 1975 by
Dave Harbour

Published by
STACKPOLE BOOKS
Cameron and Kelker Streets
Harrisburg, Pa. 17105

Printed in the U.S.A.

Library of Congress Cataloging in Publication Data

Harbour, Dave, 1920-
    Hunting the American wild turkey.

    1. Turkey hunting. I. Title.
SK325.T8H37   799.2'48'61   74-31449
ISBN 0-8117-1863-2

Contents

Contents (Continued)

Contents (Continued)

young hen, the young gobbler. Reading the flock flush. Constructing blinds. Calling young birds. Random calling. How to shoot a turkey that finds you. Tips on learning fall turkey calling right.

Foreword

To me, the American wild turkey is the epitome of complete majesty, unmatched grace, total nobility, striking beauty, pure wildness, and unsurpassed cunning and wisdom. He is both my beloved friend and respected opponent of forest and field —the most worthy and challenging adversary I have ever had the privilege to duel.

I hunt this magnificent and respected adversary with a clear conscience and with apology to no man. First, he is a far better warrior than I am, defeating me far more often than I defeat him. I pursue him not for that occasional and hard-won victory, but for the excitement of our duel in remote swamps and on lonesome mountainsides, for the thrill of seeing his great tracks etched in sand, glimpsing his black blur in golden oaks, then hearing the boom of his alarm putt and winged escape. These are the magic ingredients which stir the caveman corner of my soul and tempt me from the clanging anthill city into his wild and remote lairs. These are the irresistible forces which draw me like a sleepwalker down snake-infested and mosquito-laden trails in the eerie pre-dawn darkness—where yellow dawn and birdsong and gobbler thunder finally explode the birth of another dramatic and unforgettable day.

Where my respected opponent is not well established, I hunt him with hypnotized eyes and shaking camera. But where he is entrenched in goodly numbers, I have no hesitation in challenging him with bow or gun. I know that only my concern and license money, and that of other hunters, have saved this great bird from extinction and multiplied his numbers by ten-fold in the past few generations. I know that wild turkeys cannot be stockpiled, and that controlled harvesting helps prevent unnecessary losses to less merciful natural causes, such as starvation and disease. And I know that spring seasons are timed so that any gobbler I bag has already sired his young. It is for these reasons that I can hunt the bird I love and respect above all others with complete satisfaction and no reservation.

I have attempted, I hope with reasonable success, to make this the most complete book on turkey hunting ever written, the most important legacy I would like to leave those who follow me. The book seems to cover every point which the new hunter, the occasional hunter, and the experienced hunter need to know. Yet it strives to be a "no fluff" book—one which covers every point all these hunters need to know, but not one which they don't.

The book's first objective is to paint the thrilling rewards of turkey hunting discovered during my more than forty years of challenging America's King of Birds. Accordingly, the book includes detailed accounts of my most exciting duels with the four races of U.S. turkeys from coast to coast. Every unpredictable duel is different, and the different lessons from each should benefit other hunters. It is also my hope that readers will enjoy the same suspense and the same thrills that I did as they walk with me through these memorable hunts—and that some day they can duplicate them.

The book's second objective is to provide the most complete and up-to-date advice possible on modern equipment and tactics for turkey hunting—in the spring and in the fall—

and with both gun and bow. Great emphasis is placed on turkey calls and calling. For the new and occasional hunter, proven and easy-to-learn calling techniques are explained in clear and easy-to-follow words. And for the experienced hunter, new and unusual tricks for fooling the craftiest old gobblers are also detailed. A chapter is even included on pay-off tactics for hunting turkeys without a call.

The book also includes condensed planning data which can save the hunter many hours in planning his turkey hunts. One chart indicates states with highest turkey populations, plus the kinds of seasons (spring or fall or both) usually held. And an Appendix lists addresses of all state game and fish agencies to contact for latest hunting information. It also lists top turkey hunting areas in each state found in no other single document. And most chapters of the book describe in detail other turkey hunting areas which are exceptionally good. Finally, the book covers thought provoking predictions by the nation's leading turkey experts on the outlook for turkey hunting in the year 2000, plus specific actions which must be taken to save the wild turkey—and the great sport of hunting itself.

Deep appreciation is expressed to those many fellow hunters, to wildlife biologists of the various state game and fish agencies, and to leading critics on outdoor publication staffs, who reviewed and suggested improvements in the manuscript. Finally, I am particularly indebted to *Sports Afield* for permission to use substantial selections from my works previously published in that magazine.

CHAPTER 1

Getting Ready For The Turkey Hunt: Quick-Look Facts To Help You Prepare And Plan

I yelped and the old tom roared back with a passionate gobble. Then he topped the ridge in full strut shining like polished copper in the new sun. His great chestnut tail was fanned wide. His mammoth wings drooped to the ground. Tints of greens and golds sparkled from the broad blackness of his breast—and his long thick beard almost touched the ground. Then "VTT-VRR-OO-MM-I" came the sound of the booming strut. Then another "GIL-OBBLE-OBBLE-OBBLE! GIL-OBBLE-OBBLE-OBBLE!"

An opera like this, played on a remote forest stage in the soft light of the new sun, is almost more than a man can bear. How he wishes that such magic moments could last forever. And, in a sense they do. For they will be relived a hundred times in a hundred places: in the wait for dawn in other spring woods, over tall cool drinks on summer evenings, and in the quietness of long nights when men dream. These en-

13

U.S. WILD TURKEY SEASONS AND POPULATIONS

Courtesy Penn's Woods Products and Professor Henry Mosby

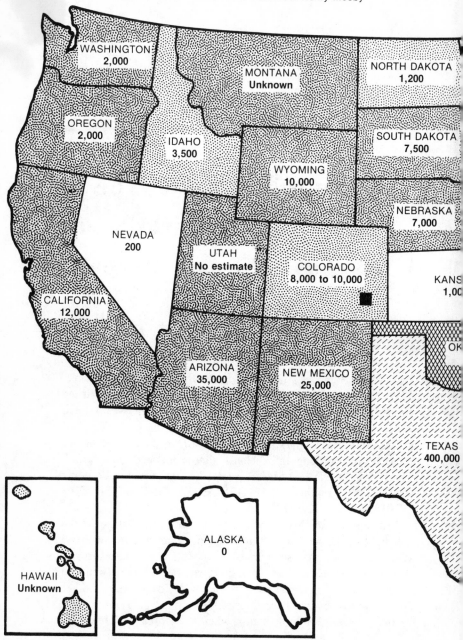

WASHINGTON
2,000

OREGON
2,000

MONTANA
Unknown

NORTH DAKOTA
1,200

IDAHO
3,500

SOUTH DAKOTA
7,500

WYOMING
10,000

NEBRASKA
7,000

NEVADA
200

UTAH
No estimate

COLORADO
8,000 to 10,000

KANS
1,00

CALIFORNIA
12,000

ARIZONA
35,000

NEW MEXICO
25,000

OK

TEXAS
400,000

HAWAII
Unknown

ALASKA
0

Note: Information is approximate—check State Game and Fish Agencies for latest information when planning hunts (see addresses in Appendix I)

chanting and enduring moments are the real rewards of turkey hunting.

Yes, the man who discovers the many-splendored thrills of hunting America's King of Birds is lucky indeed—even if he never pulls the trigger or fires an arrow. But this need not be any turkey hunter's fate. An occasional trophy tom is an attainable objective for any man—if he is willing to devote a reasonable amount of time to learning the habits of his quarry and to mastering the tactics required to duel him. A clear-cut pattern for accomplishing these tasks will be found in the pages which follow.

U.S. WILD TURKEYS: DISTRIBUTION AND WHERE-TO-HUNT INFORMATION

The wild turkey has made a striking comeback throughout the nation. From a point of near-extinction a few generations ago, our wild turkey population today has soared to more than a million birds. Illustration 1 accompanying this chapter shows turkey populations in each state and the types of hunting seasons usually held in each. And Appendix 1 in the back of the book lists state agencies to contact for up-to-date hunting information—plus good hunting areas in each state. In addition, many exceptionally fine turkey hunting areas will be pinpointed in following chapters along with information on how to hunt them. All this should help you plan productive turkey trips anywhere from coast to coast.

The amazing comeback of the wild turkey is due primarily to two factors: the dedicated efforts of competent wildlife managers and biologists in our state and federal agencies—and to the financing of their work by hunters who buy licenses and pay excise taxes on arms, ammunition, and archery equipment.

Description of U.S. Turkeys

All U.S. Wild turkeys look somewhat similar to dark domestic strains, except that they are thinner, more stream-lined, and far more wild and alert looking. All four races

The Eastern turkey is almost completely dark chestnut and shines like polished copper in the sunlight.

usually appear black at a distance. At close range, black and white wing feathers, generally chestnut tails, and copper body feathers tinted with iridescent greens, purples, golds, and even reds become conspicuous. Main tail feathers of the Eastern turkey, and its close cousin the Florida turkey, terminate in a wide black band, then a tip of *dark buff* or *brown*. Rump feathers are *dark chestnut* sometimes tipped with a velvety black band. The Rio Grande turkey of Texas looks very much like the Eastern turkey except that its rump feathers are

The Merriam turkey of the West is a beautiful bird with white or creme rump feathers and a tail-tip band of the same color.

lighter, more of a *cinnamon buff* color. The principal turkey of the West, the Merriam, has a striking *cream* or *white* rump and a *white*-tipped tail. Because of this coloration, the Eastern hunter could easily believe that the first Merriam he sees is a domestic turkey. But when he tries to close to shooting range, he'll quickly discover that the Merriam is far from tame.

Gobbler Identification

In all four races, gobblers are far larger than hens. Adult gobblers usually weigh between 15 and 20 pounds and occasionally a few pounds more. Adult hens weigh from 6

The Florida turkey is similar in appearance to his cousin, the Eastern turkey, except his feathers are less barred. The Rio Grande turkey is also similar to the Eastern turkey except its rump feathers are lighter, more of a cinnamon buff.

to 12 pounds. The heads of gobblers are larger than those of hens, and less feathered. And they vary in color from white, to blue, to red, or some hue between, depending on the season of the year and mood of the turkey. In mating season the head of an old gobbler is most often pale sky-blue with a white crown. Gobblers also have pronounced upper neck wattles, especially in the spring, and distinct spurs which hens lack. If any hunter spots a big tom strutting, identification is no problem. The fluffed-out feathers, drooping wings, and wide-fanned tail of a strutting gobbler make him stand out like a neon sign. However, during most other situations in spring and fall, new hunters will find positive gobbler identification difficult. When hunting a gobbler-only area, it's important to adopt one criterion for identifying any tom which is not strutting: *"Shoot only when you see a beard!"*

The importance of making this gobbler identification rule a strict discipline *before* the hunt begins will be understood by the new hunter when he suddenly finds himself within gun or bow range of his first turkey or flock of turkeys. Even then, he'll find that most wild turkeys look largely alike, especially if they are in shadows or brush. Even the beard of an old non-strutting tom is often difficult or impossible to spot until the big bird turns sideways to the hunter in good light. Before firing his gun or bow, the hunter must often wait, motionless and with great patience, in order to make out even this long beard.

Since turkeys hatch out in the summer, the beards of young gobblers are rarely visible the following fall. By spring, however, they are likely to have short but visible beards. And from the following fall on their beards are usually 4 to 12 inches long. Not more than one turkey hen out of a hundred will have a beard—and that rare beard on a hen usually is fine and difficult to see. Therefore, if the hunter spots any easy-to-see beard, he can be reasonably sure that its owner is a gobbler. Besides, authorities in most turkey states would not prosecute a hunter who bags a bearded hen by accident in a "gobbler only" hunting area.

The new hunter may read or hear about other methods of gobbler identification. Literature published by some state game and fish agencies points out that during non-strutting hours, most hens are on nests during spring seasons; therefore, any turkeys the hunter sees moving about will probably be toms. This is factual information but it should never be used as the sole criterion for spring gobbler identification. Some nesting hens may be moving about to feed, water, and to visit gobblers, and non-nesting hens are usually moving about. And, of course, all turkeys move about all day in the fall. Other literature suggests that gobblers can be identified by their "large size, large bluish-red heads and by their long leg spurs." When alone, any wild turkey will look big as an ostrich to the new hunter. Spotting the spurs on the biggest gobbler, even at easy shotgun or bow range, is almost impossible for anyone. And when a turkey or a flock of turkeys is moving about in the shadows or brush, head color and size are also difficult

"Look for that beard!" is the cardinal rule for gobbler identification. A careful look at the bird in the foreground will reveal a short beard. He's a young gobbler.

markings for an inexperienced hunter to detect. Identification clues such as these may be helpful in deciding which turkeys to examine more closely, but the positive sighting of that beard should be the primary criterion used by every new hunter for identifying a non-strutting gobbler.

The preceding non-technical description of U.S. turkeys and tips on gobbler identification have purposely been brief

Two-year-old gobblers usually have spurs about a half-inch long. Those of old gobblers are usually more than an inch long, sharp-pointed and often curved.

and confined to what the new turkey hunter needs to know—for the sole subject of this book is *hunting*. For an excellent detailed and technical description of all wild turkeys, including those of Mexico, read A. W. Scorger's *The Wild Turkey, Its History and Domestication,* published by The University of Oklahoma Press. Mannerisms and habits of U.S. wild turkeys which *are* important to hunters will be discussed along with hunting tactics in following chapters.

BEST GUNS AND LOADS FOR TURKEY HUNTING

Any shotgun is a good turkey gun when you have your bird in sure range with a clear shot at his head and neck. But this is not always possible. Ranges can be hard to judge, and occasionally the hunter's only option is a body shot. For these reasons, most old turkey pros prefer a twelve-gauge shotgun and heavy loads.

Although many turkeys are bagged with small shotguns, that larger and more dense shot pattern thrown by the twelve makes the effectiveness of every shot more certain. The 3-inch twelve gauge is an even more lethal gobbler gun than the standard 2¾-inch twelve for the same reason. The hunter just embarking on the trail of toms should not fear the slight additional weight and kick of the twelve, even the 3-inch twelve. Packing a little extra weight and taking a little extra kick for one or two shots is cheap insurance to pay for that higher probability of success when the chips are down.

Full-choke side-by-side or over-and-under doubles, pumps, or automatics are all good gobbler guns. The gas-operated automatics, such as the Remington 1100, shoot with less recoil than the other guns and are therefore good choices for the hunter who is of slight build. And a selective firing double gives the hunter an important first-shot option of small shot for the head and neck of a standing gobbler, or large shot for the body of a running or flying gobbler. Other differences between basic shotgun types are of little real importance in turkey hunting.

The new or occasional turkey hunter may not want to put out the money for a new turkey gun—and he rarely needs to. Good used twelves of the type just described are available in most gun shops and sporting goods stores at half to three-quarters the price of new guns. When buying a used shotgun, however, it is important to be sure that it is guaranteed against defects and to make certain it always fires (with both barrels in the case of doubles) before heading for your turkey area.

The old gobbler especially is armor plated by heavy back and wing bones and his breast is thick. However, a few small shot in the head or neck will kill him cleanly. When using a single-barrel gun and calling turkeys, a close first shot at the head and neck is likely and desirable, so a #4 or #6 in the chamber is best. Second and third shots, if needed, will usually be at flying or running birds and #2's or BB's are best shot sizes. These larger shots are also best for the chamber when stalking, and only running or flying shots are likely. Number 4 buckshot may be the best load when shotgunning for deer and turkeys at the same time.

When purchasing shells, the new hunter should take out additional turkey killing insurance by selecting magnum or maximum-load shells with plastic shot collars, or "protectors." Magnum loads contain the maximum amount of pellets and powder, and plastic shot collars insure the maximum number of *effective* pellets in the target area. The hunter should also check the way his shotgun patterns all loads, and consider this factor before making his final selection of shells. For example, some barrels will pattern #4's best and others will pattern #6's best. In areas where rifle hunting is permitted and the hunter desires to use a rifle, a small caliber rifle in the .22

Total camouflage, including face and hands, is of overriding importance when hunting the sharp-eyed turkey.

Magnum to .243 caliber range is an ideal choice. The combination rifle-shotgun is also a good turkey gun in areas where it is legal.

BEST BOWS AND ARROWS FOR THE TURKEY HUNT

More and more of the nation's million and a quarter bowhunters are turning to the challenging sport of turkey hunting. And those that have know that the wild turkey is *big game,* and they select their bow tackle accordingly. No new hunter should settle for any turkey hunting bow with a draw weight of less than 45 pounds, the minimum also usually required for deer hunting. One good bow will last you a lifetime and you can use it for all game, big and small, as well as for turkeys. And any bowhunter is a better shot if he shoots one bow all the time. So, it pays to buy a *good* bow with big game killing power.

Although many of the finest turkey bowhunters I know are instinctive or bare-bow shooters, many others use a bow sight. I'm a sight man, and have taken three gobblers with a compound bow set at 55 pounds and equipped with a sight with three posts set at 20, 30, and 40 yards. If you're just starting out, try both shooting methods and decide early on which way you want to go. Then practice faithfully using the same shooting method you'll be using when you draw on your first turkey.

Be sure your arrows are matched to your bow and shoot well from it; and buy one set of identical arrows for both practice and hunting. Arrows which accommodate convertapoint or screw-in type heads are ideal, since they allow you to practice and hunt with the same arrows and with heads of exactly the same weights. Multi-headed big game broadheads are as essential for turkey hunting as they are for deer hunting, and must be kept *razor sharp.*

SHAPING UP FOR THE TURKEY HUNT

The hunter should become intimately familiar with any new gun or bow prior to turkey hunting with it. Many split second opportunities to take turkeys are lost through being unfamiliar with a new bow or bow sight—or fumbling too long to find the safety on a new gun, trying to fire with the safety on, or failing to fully close a pump-action gun. The hunter should shoot his new gun or bow many times to become intimately and instinctively familiar with its operation. Sustained practice on the skeet, trap, or archery range is a quick and effective avenue for attaining this basic proficiency.

The hunter should also devote at least one afternoon prior to his first turkey hunt to determining exactly where a new shotgun projects its shot pattern in relation to the aiming point. Large pasteboard boxes or newspaper pages are adequate targets for making this determination. Choke devices raise front sights and often cause guns to shoot low. If the hunter discovers this before the hunt, he will have no problem when the chips are down, for he will *know* where to hold.

EQUIPMENT AND CAMOUFLAGE REQUIREMENTS

Always equip yourself with comfortable, drab, and noiseless clothing. No gun or bowhunter can concentrate properly on turkey hunting if he is uncomfortable. The typical hunt is chilly during early mornings and warm during mid-afternoons. On the other hand, the day of the hunt may prove to be very hot or very cold. Therefore, the wise turkey hunter will tote along both cold and hot weather clothing on both spring and fall hunts. His cold weather clothing should include light and warm thermal underwear plus waterproof boots and wool socks. Where legal, both cold and warm weather clothing should be of a dark camouflage color, for the turkey is a sharp-eyed bird. The old gobbler is also a sharp-eared bird, and canvas or duck trousers or coats which broadcast noise each time they are scraped by brush or tree limbs will handicap even the stealthiest hunter. All outer garments should be made of noiseless cotton, wool, or other soft material. And clanking key chains, loose coins, and other noisy objects belong on no turkey hunt. Both gun and bowhunters should beware of buying low-priced imported camouflage clothing which is too light

Big guns and heavy loads gave the author and his two hunting companions these big Colorado Merriams.

to start with and which fades even lighter after repeated laundering.

Proper camouflage of face and hands is also of vital importance. Excellent gloves and face masks, made of camouflage netting, are distributed by Penns Woods Products, Delmont, Pa. Grease camouflage paints, available at most archery stores, are preferred by some old turkey pros, for paint is always in place; it never interferes with vision; and it can't snag when you're easing through brush or getting ready to shoot. Even the turkey hunter's gun barrel or bow should be covered with camouflage or dull black tape, which is also available at most archery stores.

A good compass is essential on most turkey hunts in order to navigate in the woods before dawn and on cloudy or foggy days. Small lightweight binoculars are also valuable for identifying distant turkeys. Turkey calls will be discussed thoroughly in the following chapter.

THE NATIONAL WILD TURKEY FEDERATION

Every turkey hunter should be familiar with the only nonprofit organization in the country which is dedicated solely to improving turkey hunting for this and future generations— and he should support it. This organization is the National Wild Turkey Federation. The author's enthusiastic support of this worthy Federation upon its conception is indicated by the following letter to Tom Rodgers, its President.

Mr. Thomas F. Rodgers, President
THE NATIONAL WILD TURKEY FEDERATION
P.O. Box 467
Edgefield, S.C.   29824

Dear Tom:

I'm enclosing my tax-deductible check for a Life Membership in THE NATIONAL WILD TURKEY FEDERATION.
As you may know, this is a large amount of money to donate, and I thought about it a long time. The reasons I'm buying a life membership are these: (1) I know that the real objective of the Federation is to improve wild turkey hunting for this and future generations, and it's important to me that those who follow us will know the same thrills of turkey hunting that we oldtimers know today; (2) I have known you and many members of the advisory board long enough to know that you will do your utmost to see that the Federation prospers and accomplishes its worthy objective; and (3) I know that these early days will be tough ones for the Federation, and especially for you, since it will take time for the Federation to become well known and to secure enough members to sustain itself financially. Therefore, it is my hope that my buying a life membership will encourage others who love turkey hunting, and who are able, to do the same NOW— when the Federation needs their support the most.

Feel free to use my testimony in encouraging others to join your worthy organization—and the best of luck!

Sincerely yours,
Dave Harbour

Since this letter was written, thousands of gun and bow hunters, as well as scores of the nation's top wild turkey biologists, researchers, and managers, have joined The Wild Turkey Federation. Those unable to buy life memberships, bought charter memberships, or annual memberships. As a result, the organization is growing fast and speaks out for all hunters on issues affecting the perpetuation of the wild turkey and turkey hunting.

In addition, *Turkey Call,* the Federation's magazine, is now a national forum for the exchange of important and interesting facts on turkeys and every issue contains helpful hints on turkey hunting. Every hunter, not already a member, should support this organization now.

CHAPTER 2

Spring Gobbler Calling Made Easy

Spring turkey calling has long been surrounded by an air of mystery and difficulty—and no wonder! Most old pros are not anxious to admit their art is easy to learn. Using human words to describe turkey language appears to be a monumental task—especially since turkeys use scores of different combinations of basic calls and no two turkeys sound exactly the same. (Even a turkey hen cannot memorize the individual calls of each of her poults.) And it's true that any turkey call is likely to sound different to different people, for most of us are "tone-sensitive" or "tone-deaf" in widely varying degrees.

In spite of the above, calling spring gobblers can be easily taught and easily learned. This task is attainable because of two important and often overlooked facts. First, it is possible to forget all the many confusing kinds of turkey talk and to bag gobblers in the spring by concentrating on only *two* simple calls; and second, anyone can easily learn to reproduce these two calls accurately enough to do the job—even if he is completely tone deaf. That is, he can if he follows the simple instructions in this book.

THE BASIC TURKEY CALLING INSTRUMENTS

The old wing bone yelper, snuffbox, and leaf, used by our pioneer turkey hunters of yesteryear are rarely seen any more. There are few experts left who can call with their own voices. Even the wooden matchbox scratched with a sharp pocket-knife is now only a legendary caller, for they make matchboxes out of paper these days—a fact I heard most vehemently condemned by an ancient West Virginian as he sat on a stump trying to use a new-fangled box. In reality, the sleek modern calls are more effective than the old ones. But each of these has its limitations as well as capabilities, and appreciating them is important if you are thinking about talking turkey.

Box Callers

The most popular of these are hollow boxes with handles hinged to one end. Calls are made by sliding the handle across the thin rim of the box. These are the easiest of all calls to learn to use, for they are "pre-tuned" at the factory so that a long stroke with the handle across the top of the box produces a fairly realistic "yelp," while a short stroke produces

A typical box turkey call. For those who are tone-deaf, it's easiest of all calls to use. It also has great volume and makes the most realistic cluck of any call.

With the Lynch Box call, the hunter can cluck, yelp, whine, and even gobble.

a "cluck." Gobbles can also be reproduced with some boxes. Other good boxes are operated by stroking the box edge with a separate wooden stroker. Most boxes provide greater volume and calling range than other calls. They produce almost perfect clucks, and they are ideal calls for those who are tone-deaf. Their biggest limitations are that most are large and awkward to carry—and they are not usually as effective when a turkey is close as are the quieter and softer calls. Fine boxes I've tested include the "True Tone" made by Penn's Woods Products, Delmont, Pa., the "World Champion Turkey Call" made by M. L. Lynch, P.O. Box 377, Liberty, Miss., and the "Gaskin's Box" made by Tom Gaskins, Palmdale, Fla. To produce true tones, the edges of all boxes should be rubbed with greasless blue carpenter's chalk—not plain white chalk—before each series of calls.

This is the largest turkey call in the world. It's made by Tom Gaskins of Palmdale, Florida. His regular size boxes are preferred by many pros from coast to coast.

Slate Callers

Most good slate callers are less than half as large as box callers. They consist of two units. One is a piece of slate, or a hollow sound box with slate on one side. The other is a piece of wood or corncob with a peg for stroking the slate. Both units of my favorite slate, the "Roger Latham Slate Call," made by Penn's Woods, fit together into one compact unit for easy carrying and protection of the peg. Other good slate callers include the "Jet Slate Call" made by M. L. Lynch, the "Daniel Boone Slate" by D-Boone Enterprises, P.O. Box 8, Highspire, Pa., and the "Missile Bird" by Joymere Wood Products, Georgiana, Ala. To produce perfect tones, the slates on all these calls must be roughened with sandpaper before each series of calls. The big advantages of slate calls are their compactness and ability to produce very low and soft calls,

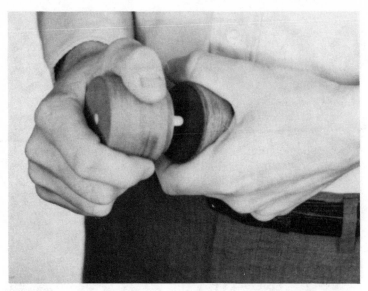

The slate turkey call is excellent for close-in calling.

both clucks and yelps. The slate is easy to learn to use. And it also can be used with reasonable effectiveness by most hunters who tend toward tone deafness, but the slate is not as foolproof in this respect as is a good box. And if a slate call gets wet, it's worthless.

Diaphragm Callers

One of the newest of turkey callers is a tiny horseshoe shaped metal disc with a thin rubber vibrator. It fits neatly into the roof of the mouth with the open end forward. The basic yelp is made by pressing the back part of the tongue against the back portion of the caller and the tip of the tongue against the teeth, then by moving air against the vibrator from deep within the chest. Using this caller, an expert can reproduce any turkey call with almost unbelievable realism. This "mouth yelper" offers other important advantages. It enables calling without body movement. It is capable of producing the softest of calls for close-in birds. And its use leaves the hunter's hands free to keep his gun in a ready position. This caller

The mouth diaphragm call or "yelper" is a superb call for those with a good musical ear. When using it, the hunter's hands are always free.

has three disadvantages. It is not capable of those loud calls often necessary to locate birds. It is a difficult call for most hunters to learn to use. And a good musical ear is required to get good tones from it. Diaphragm callers are made by Penn's Woods Products, Lynch, and by Rex Sporting Goods Company, 101 North Main Street, Atmore, Alabama.

Suction Callers Or Yelpers

Three excellent yelpers are on the market today. The "Tom Turpin Yelper," made by Penn's Woods, and the "Diamond Yelper" by Trigg Jacobs, Rt. 2, Eldorado, Ark., are fine wood and rubber reproductions of the old turkey wing bone caller. By sucking on the mouthpiece, as in the act of kissing, a realistic yelp or cluck can be made. These calls are stream-lined, compact, and can be carried on a string around the neck, or attached to a buttonhole on your hunting coat for quick and easy availability and insurance against loss. And they are not difficult calls to learn to use by the hunter with a good musical ear. The third suction-type caller is "Leon's Turkey Caller" made by LCJ Manufacturing Co., 114 Randolph St., Lexington, Va. This is a compact little box with a rubber diaphragm over one end. Calls are made by placing the dia-phragm against the lower lip and sucking air in. In the hands

Leon Johenning's box suction caller, instructional record, and Turkey Hunter's Guide are excellent hunting and calling aids.

of the expert, this is one of the most effective callers made. However, it is one of the most difficult of all calls for most hunters to learn to use. And, like the diaphragm caller, only those with a good musical ear can produce true tones with it.

Tube-Type Callers

The new tube type callers are modern versions of the old

The new tube or "pill bottle" calls are blown by placing the upper lip over the top half of the call covered with the rubber diaphragm. They are best all-around calls for yelping and close-in work, even for those with a poor musical ear.

snuffbox call. They are made of small plastic or metal pill bottles or tubes with a small hole in the bottom and half of the lid or top cut away. A thin rubber diaphragm, usually made of surgeon's glove, is stretched over the half-open top of the tube and held in place by the rim of the tube lid, or by rubber band or tape. Calls are made by cupping the bottom of the tube in both hands, and by placing the upper lip over the top of the diaphragm so that the lower lip just touches the bottom of the diaphragm. One should first learn to make the high and the low tone of the yelp by blowing and varying the amount and direction of air pressure exerted against the diaphragm. Then he must learn to run these two tones together to produce a yelp.

No caller is capable of producing a more perfect soft yelp than the tube. For most hunters, the tube is far easier to learn to use than any other caller except a box. It is unaffected by rain, and it is so small it can easily be carried in the shirt pocket or on a string around the neck. And most tone deaf hunters can learn to use it. The primary disadvantages of the tube are its lack of volume for long range calling and the difficulty many hunters have in making a realistic cluck with it. Many hunters make their own tube callers from a plastic pill container. My favorite tube caller is made by Harold Knight, Cadiz, Ky., and Dave Hale, Gracey, Ky. Other tubes are made by Penn's Woods Products and D-Boone Enterprises.

WHICH CALLER SHOULD YOU BUY?

First, most new hunters will need a good box, at least to cluck with. Also, the loud yelps capable of reproduction with a box will often make locating turkeys easier. Even if you use the box only until you get an answer and locate your gobbler, it may be well worth packing along on every hunt. By bearing down on the box, you can send calls much farther than you can with the other type callers. In the spring, this can stimulate distant gobblers to respond which would not hear the softer callers.

Second, hunters will also need one of the soft callers for close-in yelping. Which one? If you can whistle or sing a

tune well—in other words, if you have a good musical ear—
you'll probably be wisest to try a mouth diaphragm or suction
caller first. If you are tone deaf, or have a poor musical ear,
then buy a tube or slate. The mouth diaphragm can make one
of the most realistic of all soft calls, but the hunter with a
poor musical ear probably will never master this caller regardless of how much he practices. The same is true of suction
callers. But the tube or slate caller is a different matter. Most
hunters who are tone deaf can learn to use these callers effectively.

But remember this important qualification: *No general
rule on calling fits every individual hunter.* Try every type
caller you can find, then decide for yourself which one *you*
can call with best. Measure the realism of your calls with each
caller against recordings, calls by old pros, or calls of live
turkeys. This subject will be discussed in great detail later.

THE TWO ESSENTIAL SPRING CALLS AND
HOW TO LEARN THEM

No wonder many hunters think turkey calling is so difficult.
Most instructional booklets and records on the subject dive
into a complex discussion of many different basic calls—and
then, many different combinations of these. The reader or
listener is inclined to forget the whole perplexing business
when he is bombarded with the requirements to learn "yelps,"
"lost gobbler yelps," "lost hen yelps," love calls of the hen,"
"clucks of the old hen," "clucks of the young hen," "gobbler
clucks," "tree clucks," "assembly calls," "putts," "whines,"
"kee-kee runs" and on and on.

Most call manufacturers seem to be trying to scare off
prospective clients with such complicated training aids. To
compound the confusion, most instructional records reel off
the many different turkey calls so fast that the new hunter
has no chance to memorize one before it is drowned out by
another.

How do you learn to call turkeys in spite of all this "help"?
First, and foremost, the spring gobbler hunter should concentrate on learning only two simple calls: the cluck and the love

yelp of the hen. Being able to reproduce these two calls reasonably well can get the new hunter almost as many turkeys as an expert who can make twenty different calls with perfection.

The main call you need to learn for spring hunting is the love call or yelp of the hen. It can be made on any of the callers. This is the main call that arouses the old gobbler and brings him in—a fast and snappy series of two to six yelps. It should be made very loud (preferably with the box) to locate and get the attention of distant gobblers. It should be made very low and soft (preferably with the diaphragm, tube, suction caller, or slate, but a box will also do) when seducing a close-in bird.

There are two quick ways to learn how to make the love call of the hen. The best way is to locate a good caller who knows the value of this call and get him to tutor you. By sitting at his side and being attentive, you can usually learn to duplicate his calls in short order.

The second way to learn the love call of the hen is to buy the best available instructional records or tapes. The instructional records made by Penn's Woods Call Company, by LCJ Manufacturing Co., and by M. L. Lynch and the tape made by Harold Knight and Dave Hale, all contain good reproductions of this call. As previously indicated, this call is usually buried in a maze of other calls. But it can be memorized by taking the time to stand at the record player or tape recorder and playing this one call over and over again.

Memorizing this one basic call is all-important before heading into the spring woods. The most essential requirement is being able to reproduce the *rhythm* of the call accurately. It doesn't matter if your tone varies somewhat from that of your instructor or from that of the recording. Duff Holbrook of Atlanta and Don Thomas of Andalusia, Alabama, two of the finest callers I know, are far apart in tone. Don's tone is noticeably higher and finer than that of Duff's. Yet the rhythm of their calling is the same; and they are equally lethal when it comes to eradicating spring gobblers. This is a key point for the new caller to always bear in mind. Don't fret because your *tone* is a bit different from that of the record or

INSTRUCTION RECORD NO. 2 **33⅓ R.P.M.**

famous
wild
turkey
hunters
teach you

HOW TO CALL WILD TURKEY

THE EXPERTS

HARVEY GRAYBILL — 1970 Pa. State Champion
ROGER LATHAM — Mr. Turkey Himself
E. L. WISOR — Expert of the Slate
R. W. BAILEY — One of the Leading
    Authorities in the World
DR. LEROY UTT — Sweet Sounding Yelper
THE WILD TURKEY — Best of all with the Yelp,
    Cluck, Purr, Gobble, etc.

$2⁴⁹

Penn's Woods Products, Inc., Delmont, Pa. 15626

Listening to good instructional records is the quickest way to learn the basic turkey calls. The newest "expert's" record is distributed by Penn's Woods Products.

that of your instructor. All that counts is how you sound to a *gobbler*. Master the *rhythm* of the call and you'll do well enough.

Wayne Bailey, another expert caller and North Carolina's top turkey biologist puts it this way: "The important thing is to get the tempo of the call imbedded in your mind. Don't worry so much about tone. After all, no two turkeys sound exactly the same." I lost my old reliable box caller in New York one spring. The only replacement I could find was a Japanese imitation of my box, and its tone was far lower and coarser than any I had ever heard come from any box—or turkey. Yet, the rhythm of the call was right and the first gobbler that heard the Japanese-tuned notes came running to it hell bent for election!

Yes, memorizing the one simple call just described, with particular attention to the rhythm of the yelps in each call series, will arm you well enough to go out and bag a spring gobbler. But you can increase your odds by also mastering the simple "cluck." This call is deadly when you get within range of an old tom still on the roost. It will start him gobbling and make him fly down in your direction. This call is even easier to learn than the yelp, particularly when using a box. Many hunters who use a soft call for close-in yelping carry a box along primarily to cluck with. Clucks can also be easily learned from listening to an old pro—or to an instructional record or tape. For advanced training in both yelping and clucking, also work with *live* turkeys whenever possible (See Chapters 10 and 12).

UNDERSTANDING THE SPRING GOBBLER

Locating and calling up your spring gobbler will prove far easier and more fun if you understand the reason for spring seasons and the habits and passions of your long-bearded quarry at this time of the year. In southern Florida, spring gobbler hunts begin in early March. They begin in late March or early April in most other southern states. In more northern states, such as the Virginias, Pennsylvania, New York, Wyoming, and Colorado, they begin in mid- or late April or in May. These seasons are staggered in such a delightful way that it is actually possible to hunt spring gobblers somewhere in the country for almost three full months each year.

In any good turkey area, there are many more gobblers than required for reproduction needs. Additionally spring gobbler seasons are usually held during only a short portion of the mating season. This provides further insurance that spring seasons will not interfere with reproduction. Once deposited, the sperm cells survive in a hen long enough to fertilize all eggs in the first clutch and even long enough to fertilize the second clutch if the first is destroyed and she must re-nest. It also has been found that removal of excess toms during spring hunts may even improve reproduction by reducing interference with nesting hens. Many states have held spring gobbler hunts through the past decade and during this same period their turkey populations have risen to new highs. For these reasons, spring gobbler hunting does not threaten turkey populations anywhere.

In the spring, old gobblers tend to spread out. Each seeks to establish his own domain. There he frequently shatters the woods with his thundering gobbles, especially in the early morning. He does this to announce his presence to hens and to warn other gobblers to stay out of his territory. These booming gobbles, which can be heard nearly a mile away on quiet mornings, plus the fact that gobblers are well distributed in most spring woods, makes their location easy on most spring mornings. But there are exceptions. On exceptionally windy mornings, all or most gobblers in any area may remain silent. This means that the sharp hunter will plan to devote several days to his spring gobbler hunt to increase his odds for being in the woods during at least a couple of good gobbling mornings.

Some gobblers will gobble often and with great fervor, sometimes from the first crack of dawn until mid- or late-morning. These are usually exceptionally love-sick old birds that have no hens nearby. These are the easiest of all gobblers to locate and call up. *The most mediocre of callers can call up such a tom, as long as he calls from a reasonably good position and doesn't call too often.* Gobblers with a number of hens roosting nearby may gobble only a couple of times at first light or they may not gobble at all. But with reasonably good calling, these old toms can also be excited, made to gobble and called up later in the morning after their hens have departed. Many new hunters don't realize this and foolishly quit hunting by mid-morning.

Locating Spring Gobblers

Being in promising turkey country at first light in the morning and listening for gobbles from strategic points is the surest way to locate a springtime tom. In mountains or hill country, remember that you can hear much further from high ridgetops. One top tactic is to locate promising ridges with roads along the top, then to drive the ridgetops stopping each half-mile or so to listen. An even better tactic is to climb a remote ridge in roadless country, then to walk the top and listen. Each time you stop after daylight and fail to hear a gobble, query the forest with a loud hen love yelp. If there's a gobbler within hearing distance, this will often stimulate a booming reply.

In flat country, remember that you can hear and be heard much further across open clearings or lightly timbered country than you can in thick forested areas. As you walk, also watch for turkey tracks or for scratched out areas in leaves. If fresh turkey sign like this is noted, it means that turkeys are probably close by. If you don't hear a gobble from such an area early in the morning, it is probably because the old gobbler has a harem of hens with him. *Return to the area in mid- or late-morning and call. By then, the old tom's hens will probably be gone and you'll have an excellent chance of stimulating him to gobble.*

Finally, utilize each late afternoon of your hunt to increase your odds for locating gobblers. In most states, spring gobbler hunting is allowed only until 10 a.m., 11 a.m., or 12 noon. However, it is legal to return to the woods without your gun or bow and to scout for birds in the afternoon. Gobblers often sound off very late, usually around or just after sundown, when they fly up to their roost—and a gobble with your box or even a honk on the old car horn is a neat way to make them gobble then. So, drive along a back road during these choice late hours and stop and gobble or honk at half-mile intervals. If you are lucky enough to locate a roosting tom, you'll usually have it made. Just mark the area well and be within two or three hundred yards of the roost area at daylight the next morning. Then follow the calling suggestions which follow.

BEST SPOTS TO CALL FROM . . .
   CONCEALMENT . . .
      SEDUCING THE EAGER GOBBLER, THE
      PASSIVE TOM . . .
         WHEN AND WHERE TO SHOOT

We'll assume now that you are armed with both a good

box and one of the soft callers; that you have learned to reproduce the simple cluck and two-to-six yelp love call of the
hen; and that you have just heard a thundering gobble rattle
through the woods. You're now down to the nitty-gritty
climax of the spring gobbler hunt. How do you handle it?

First and foremost, keep your cool. Estimate the position
of the bird, his approximate distance from you and study
the terrain with utmost care. Your entire energies should now
be devoted to selecting the best possible spot to call from.
Your decision, however, should be swift as well as thorough,
for the old tom may be moving away from you—or he may
soon quit gobbling.

In making your decision on the best spot to call from,
keep three important factors in mind. First, in mountainous or
hilly country, it is difficult to call a gobbler downhill, but it is
usually easy to make him come to you *if you call from the
same contour the bird is on or from one above him.* Second,
in this type country, the old tom may approach you from
uphill even if he must make a wide circle to do so. Third, in
any kind of country, it is very difficult to call an old tom
across a stream or even a brushy bottom.

In other words, if cover permits, quickly sneak to a calling
spot on the same ridge or side of a stream or bottom the
gobbler is on, and on the same contour the gobbler is on or
one just above. Try to get within two or three hundred yards
of the bird, if you are sure you can do so without being observed by your quarry. Then look for a good hiding spot at
that point. Build a quick blind, or conceal yourself reasonably
well before calling. It is best to select a spot from which you
can see only 30 or 40 yards, for if you can see further, the
sharp-eyed old tom can also see *you* further, and is likely to
detect you before you detect him. I like to kneel with a bush,
or the trunk of a large tree or a stump between my position
and the direction I expect the bird to come from. When bowhunting and time permits, I like to build a quick blind.

The eyesight of an old tom is almost unbelievable. It has
been estimated as effective as a man's when looking through
high power binoculars. (See Chapter 8) For this reason,
all body movement must be held to a minimum. To do this,

place your gun or bow and your callers within easy reach. If the bird is still on the roost, use only clucks until he flies down. After that, the cardinal rule is to yelp just loud enough for the old tom to hear you and to call infrequently.

The old tom will hear your first call. From that moment on, he will know *exactly* where you are. Have no doubt about this. The remainder of your calls are not necessary to help him locate you. They are only necessary to entice him to come to you. If you call too loud or too often thereafter, the old gobbler will probably think you are excited enough to come to him as a well-mannered hen should. And he'll usually wait, or "hang up" at the spot he's gobbling from. Your job is to play coy, to let him know that there's a chance he *might* make the grade, but that he'll have to *travel* to do it.

You can sometimes judge what a particular gobbler will do by the way he answers your first call. If he comes right back with an ear-shattering gobble or two, it's likely that he will come in rapidly. Make no answering call, but listen for his next gobble to determine the direction he's moving. If you hear nothing for a couple of minutes, pick up your gun or bow and be still and ready, for he's probably boring in. If his next gobble indicates he is circling in your direction or moving slowly toward you, this is the time to call again softly. Give him a very soft and short (two or three yelp) call, and pick up your gun or bow immediately whether he answers or not. He'll probably arrive shortly.

The uninitiated turkey hunter would assume that an old tom is in the bag once he steps out in plain view and in easy shotgun or bow range. But unless the hunter is really cool, such a gobbler still has a long life expectancy. In less time than it takes to bat an eye, an old tom can spot a poorly hidden hunter, or one that moves, and put himself behind the nearest tree before the amazed hunter can react. The trick is to freeze with the gun or bow pointed generally in the direction you think the tom will come from—then to raise your gun to shooting position, or draw your bow only when the bird is in sure range and when his head is behind a bush, tree, or his strutting tail. If hunting with a shotgun, shoot at the upper neck just below the head the moment it reappears. If bowhunting, do the same if the range is point-blank and you're good enough. For most of us who bowhunt turkeys, a neck shot, however, is rarely an acceptable gamble. Especially when the range is 30 or 40 yards, aiming at the old tom's vital body cavity will up any bowhunter's odds for scoring. (See Chapter 16.)

When an old gobbler fails to answer your call, or answers it half-heartedly, or hangs up where he's gobbling from, the chances are high that he has hens with him. You can rarely compete with hens successfully, but as mentioned earlier, you can take him when the hens are gone. In this situation, you have two options. One is to stay at your calling spot, to be patient, and to call softly at ten or fifteen minute intervals. You may have to wait two or three hours but there's a good chance that the old tom's hens will eventually leave and that he will then come to court you. The other option is preferred by most experts. It's to move and to call from other strategic points with the objective of locating a more cooperative bird. If this fails, the hunter then returns to the area where he heard the first bird and tries to seduce him later in the morning.

There may be times when you are unknowingly competing with a hen on the other side of your gobbler. In this situation, the old gobbler may well move away from you to the vicinity of the hen, then further off to another. He may move a great distance and not come back. And you may return to camp unfairly blaming your lousy calling. Also, young gobblers will sometimes gobble when they are still too young to be really interested in the love call of any hen. So, don't fret because you fail to call up a particular gobbler or even a string of several birds. The finest callers strike out frequently. Just keep working and before long you'll run into an eager old tom that will run over you. From that point on, you'll have complete confidence in your ability to call—and you'll be a dedicated spring gobbler hunter.

Spring gobbler calling really is all this easy! Realizing this is the first important step in becoming a successful turkey hunter. Of course, there are a lot of sophisticated wrinkles which can also up your odds for a gobbler with gun or bow. You'll find these, plus a lot of exciting turkey hunting adventures in the chapters which follow.

CHAPTER 3

Chart Study Of Spring Gobbler Hunting

During a single spring hunt a few years ago, I recorded data on gobbler behavior, hunting tactics, and hunting hotspots in six eastern states: Florida, Alabama, South Carolina, Georgia, Virginia, and Pennsylvania. My extensive and educational safari, which began in Florida on 7 March and which ended in Pennsylvania on 20 May, involved leaping from the sack before 3:30 a.m. on 35 hunting days, hunting during all legal hours each day, and listening for gobblers and scouting during the remainder. The charts and explanatory notes which follow should give readers more interesting and useful information on spring gobblers and spring gobbler hunting.

First chart indicates the types and number of encounters with gobblers which I experienced, and which other hunters might expect, in eastern states today. It also brings several key questions into focus: Why was I able to work only 28 of the 65 gobblers heard? Why was I able to call only 10 of the 28 gobblers worked into shooting range? And why did I bag only 5 of these? All these questions and many others

OVER-ALL SUMMARY OF 6-STATE HUNT
(March, April, and May 1972)

State Hunted	Days Hunted	Gobblers Heard	Gobblers Worked	Gobblers Called Into Shooting Range	Gobblers Bagged
Florida	8	11	9	4	1
Alabama	3	1	0	0	0
S. Carolina	4	5	4	1	1
Georgia	6	2	2	1	1
Virginia	9	38	9	2	1
Pennsylvania	5	8	4	2	1
Totals	35	65	28	10	5

on gobbler behavior and hunting tactics will be treated in the presentation which follows. As background information, I was hunting each area for the first time, but I had contacted local conservation officers, turkey biologists, or forest rangers for information on areas where spring turkey populations were highest, a planning step which every turkey hunter can and should take prior to hunting any country he is not familiar with.

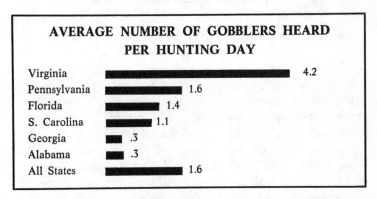

AVERAGE NUMBER OF GOBBLERS HEARD PER HUNTING DAY

Virginia	4.2
Pennsylvania	1.6
Florida	1.4
S. Carolina	1.1
Georgia	.3
Alabama	.3
All States	1.6

In all states hunted, gobbler populations as a whole are doing well, and this chart so indicates. During the 35 day hunt, I heard an average of 1.6 gobblers per day, a much higher average, oldtimers and biologists tell me, than I would have heard in the same states ten or twenty years ago. In fact, in

some of the best areas I hunted, there were no turkeys then.
This chart should not be considered a barometer of the quality
of turkey hunting in the individual states, for I hunted some
states (Alabama and Georgia) *before* the peak gobbling period
arrived, and others (Virginia and Pennsylvania) *during* the
peak gobbling period. This indicates the importance of checking on gobbling activity, when possible, just before hunting
any area. Exceptionally cold or warm weather can speed up
or delay peak gobbling activity which all states attempt to
bracket when setting their spring seasons.

Hearing spine-tingling gobbler music is, of course, the real
thrill, the real reward, the real pulled-trigger, of any spring
gobbler hunt. Finally outwitting and bagging a magnificent
gobbler, however, is also a supreme experience. And this
chart indicates further that this great moment in hunting doesn't
come without work. Never missing a moment of hunting daylight, and using hunting tactics refined from more than forty
years of gobbler chasing, it still took me an average of seven
hard hunting days to outwit each of the five gobblers I bagged.
Cheer up, new gobbler chasers. If you study this book and
are willing to work, you should be able to do at least as well!

Next chart further stresses the importance of being in the
woods at a good listening point at the first crack of dawn.
More than half of the 65 gobblers heard sounded off during
the first hour of daylight, and most of these started gobbling
just as the sky began to gray. The dim light of early morning

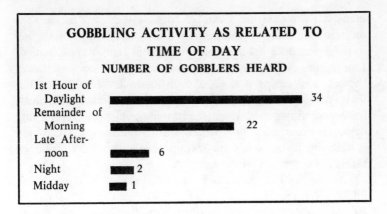

also makes it easier to close to sure calling range without spooking your sharp-eyed quarry.

As the chart also indicates, your odds for hearing gobblers are still good later in the morning. So, if you don't score early, continue to listen through legal morning shooting hours, which terminate at 10 a.m., 11 am., or 12 noon in most states. As also stressed, mid- or even late-morning can be an excellent time for calling up gobblers with harems, for their hens have usually departed by then. Only a few states allow afternoon hunting, but afternoon listening is legal. Although your odds are slim for hearing gobblers during the later hours, when one is heard, you know where he's roosting. This enables you to be close to him at first light the following morning—a tremendous advantage.

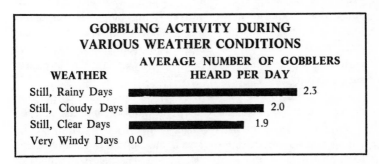

This chart confirms one gobbler hunting truth which even

many old pros are not aware of because they stay in the sack on rainy mornings: gobblers are often very active on rainy days. I heard 23 gobblers on the ten still rainy days I hunted! I heard few during real downpours, but many between heavy showers and during periods of light-to-moderate rainfall. Gobbling activity was about equally good on cloudy and clear, little-wind days; but I didn't hear a gobbler on very windy days, an observation compatible with a recent South Carolina gobbler behavior study indicating the most active gobblers rarely gobble when winds are high.

In view of the above and since changes in wind speed are difficult to forecast, it pays to hunt *every* morning. My standard gobbler hunting gear includes a pocket-size disposable plastic raincoat and a waterproof plastic bag in which to carry my box call and chalk.

LISTENING POINTS THAT PAID OFF

GOBBLERS HEARD FROM HIGH LISTENING POINTS NEAR CUT-OVER AREAS, CLEARINGS OR FIELDS ████████████████████████████ 83%

HEARD FROM OTHER AREAS █████ 17%

Hearing a gobbler is the first order of business on any spring gobbler hunt—and this depends heavily upon selecting promising spots to listen from. As this chart so clearly indicates, one of the most productive, if not the most productive listening spot is one which is both *HIGH* and *NEAR* old cut-over areas, clearings, or fields. Fifty-four of the sixty-five gobblers heard during my hunts were heard from precisely such listening spots.

Heavy timber or ridges between a low listening position and a gobbler often makes hearing a gobbler impossible even at ranges of a few hundred yards. On the other hand, by listening from a high ridge or knoll, the hunter is usually above such obstructions and gobblers can often be heard at ranges of a mile or more. As an added dividend, when you're above a

These are the kinds of gobblers the author studied and hunted with gun and camera. The charts and text in this chapter capsule the important lessons learned.

gobbler, you can usually reach a calling position near him much faster and easier.

Old cut-over areas, clearings, or fields are spring gobbler magnets of the first order because hens tend to nest in or near them because thick undercover in and near openings is desirable nesting and escape cover, and hens know that grasshoppers and other insects will be plentiful in such openings when their poults hatch out.

REASONS WHY 37 OF THE 65 GOBBLERS HEARD COULD NOT BE WORKED

15	quit gobbling before I could reach calling range
12	were heard while I was working other gobblers
8	were heard during illegal shooting hours
2	could not be reached because of a deep creek or river

Now, we begin the "true confessions" part of the presentation, with the hope that summarizing some of my goofs will help prevent other hunters from duplicating them. On 15

different occasions, I was unable to work gobblers I heard
because I was too slow in getting within calling range. In most
cases, this delay was due to waiting in hopes of hearing a closer
bird, and to the fact that more than half the gobblers I heard
gobbled for less than 15 minutes. From all this, I've learned
one big lesson: HEAD for that first gobbler heard *at once*
and with all possible speed. Slow down only when you feel
you may be getting close enough to spook him.

REASONS WHY 18 OF 28 ATTEMPTS TO CALL UP GOBBLERS FAILED

9	were spooked by other hunters
3	were spooked by me
2	went to competing hens
2	would not come to inferior calling positions
2	failed to come because of unknown reasons

Interference from other hunters was the probable cause
of my failure to call up 9 gobblers, or half the total number
worked; and, in 6 of these cases, the interference was by
hunters in my own party who had wandered from their own
assigned hunting areas. Obvious ways to minimize such interference are to hunt alone or to drop off each hunter in a party
at listening points at least a mile or two apart. In three cases,
I goofed by letting an approaching gobbler spot my movement.
In two, I simply was not skilled enough at calling to compete
with hens I could hear. And once I tried to call a gobbler
across a creek, and another up a slope covered with thick
brush, both of which were inexcusable mistakes. I should have
taken the time to select more favorable calling positions, those
which gobblers could walk to with reasonable ease.

REASONS WHY 5 OF 10 GOBBLERS CALLED INTO SHOOTING RANGE WERE NOT BAGGED

2	closed while I was hunting with camera
2	were missed
1	could not be positively identified

Both gobblers I missed sneaked in a good thirty minutes after their last gobble was heard—and I simply was not ready for them. My first view of one of them was eyeball to eyeball at a range of about 6 feet. I was lying on my side by a log with a tree trunk just beyond my head, and the gobbler's head and neck was bent around the trunk almost poking me in the face. Suddenly, the old tom made me out, putted and sold out. By the time I could get to my knees in shooting position, the gobbler was running, head down and below a contour, and I couldn't see him until he broke over the top and flushed a good 40 yards away. My snap shot missed. The second gobbler was standing about 10 yards behind me when I decided he wasn't coming and stood up to stretch. By the time I could pick up and point my gun, he was shooting straight through a maze of big hardwoods, one of which took my full charge of #6's.

Lessons: Remember a gobbler may come long after he last gobbles, so don't move prematurely, and stay alert. Try to see him soon enough to ease your gun up when his head is behind a tree or bush. If you're unable to get a sure head and neck shot before he explodes or runs, take your time, and don't snap shoot or try to shoot through a tree trunk!

I spotted another probable gobbler as he sneaked in easy range without gobbling or strutting, but he was always behind brush and I was unable to make positive identification by getting a clear view of his head or beard.

Now we come to a couple of *no-goof* charts. The first chart which follows outlines those exact tactics which got the three gobblers I bagged during the first hour of daylight. The second outlines those which got me the two gobblers I bagged later in the morning. Note the different approach and calling tactics used in the early shadowy hours when gobblers were still on their roosts, and those used later in the bright morning light after gobblers were on the ground. Even the first-time turkey hunter should have a good chance of scoring if he uses these same tactics.

CALLING TACTICS WHICH PRODUCED
DURING FIRST HOUR OF DAYLIGHT

(The three gobblers taken in Florida, South Carolina, and Georgia were all bagged through the use of the following simple tactics. All three were heard just after the first crack of dawn [5:30 - 6 a.m.] and bagged before 7 a.m.)

1. Pre-dawn listening from high points near old cut-over areas or fields.

2. Heading in direction of first gobbler heard with all possible speed, crossing wadable creeks and swamps as necessary.

3. Stopping about ¼ mile from bird, listening for his gobble, then closing on line about 30° to his right or left. (To minimize chance of overshooting and spooking him.)

4. Taking advantage of poor light and available cover to ease within 200-300 yards of bird's position.

5. Choosing calling position behind tree or bush and over-looking clearing or open woods—on or near same contour as gobbler—and with no streams or brushy hollows between gobbler and calling position.

6. *Clucking* softly two or three times. (In all three cases, gobbler answered from roost and continued gobbling at frequent intervals.)

7. Letting gobbler sweat and gobble. Then making one run of three or four snappy hen yelps *only* after muffled gobbles indicated bird had flown to ground.

8. Picking up gun, punching off safety, and freezing until gobbler moved into sure range. (Less than 30 minutes for all three birds.)

9. Pointing gun only when gobbler's head was behind tree or bush, and firing when head and neck reappeared.

Duplicating those simple tactics just outlined should give any new hunter odds for bagging his own gobbler in a week or less of hard hunting. And, bagging your own gobbler is, of course, far more fun, and actually easier, than having someone else call him in for you.

CALLING TACTICS WHICH PRODUCED
AFTER FIRST HOUR OF DAYLIGHT

(The two gobblers taken in Virginia and Pennsylvania were both bagged through the use of the equally simple tactics that follow. Both were first heard about 8:30 a.m. and bagged before 10 a.m. The Virginia gobbler was accompanied by another gobbler.)

1. Listening from high points near old cut-over areas or fields.

2. Heading in direction of first gobbler heard with all possible speed.

3. Stopping about ½ mile from bird, listening for his gobble, then crossing to same open hardwood ridge gobbler was on.

4. Easing down ridge toward gobbler, stopping because of bright daylight and sparse cover about 400 yards from his position.

5. Lying face down behind tree or bush on open knoll at point where climbing gobbler couldn't spot me until he topped the same knoll in easy range.

6. Making one run of three or four snappy hen yelps. (In both cases, the birds answered and continued gobbling at frequent intervals.)

7. *After 15 minutes,* making another run of three or four yelps, (The Pennsylvania gobbler answered with a double gobble, then silence, and I knew he was on his way to me. After a third run of yelps, the Virginia gobbler did the same.)

8. Picking up gun, punching off safety, and pointing it down the knoll, still in prone position.

9. Firing when gobbler's head and neck popped into view. (Less than 10 minutes after last gobble for both birds.)

These tactics are equally simple—and especially deadly on late-morning gobblers.

COMPARISON OF GOBBLERS BAGGED

	Weight	Beard Length and Shape	Spur Length and Shape	Age
Florida Gobbler	17½ lbs.	10" Tip Sharp	1¼" Sharp Straight	3 yrs.
South Carolina Gobbler	17 lbs.	10" Tip Sharp	¾" Dull Straight	2 yrs.
Georgia Gobbler	18 lbs.	10½" Tip Sharp	1¼" Sharp Straight	3 yrs.
Virginia Gobbler	20 lbs.	9¾" Tip Worn—Curly	⅞" Dull Straight	2 yrs.
Pennsylvania Gobbler	21 lbs.	8½" Tip Worn—Curly	¾" Dull Straight	2 yrs.

This last chart bears out some interesting facts on eastern gobblers. Weight is not necessarily an indication of a gobbler's age. Northern gobblers are usually heavier than southern gobblers, and because they live in ice and snow country, they usually have shorter beards with curly worn tips. The length of a gobbler's beard, in the north or south, is not necessarily an indication of his age, but the length and shape of his spurs usually are. The spurs of a two-year-old gobbler, the youngest tom which usually gobbles well, are for the most part blunt and less than an inch long, while those of a three-year-or-more-old gobbler are usually sharp pointed and more than an inch long.

CHAPTER 4

How To Float To A Spring Gobbler

The gobble boomed like a clap of thunder! Adrenalin pumped and I bounced on the seat almost upsetting the frail kayak. "Good Lord!" Duff whispered and whipped the kayak toward the dark blur of the bank. I reached for a tangle of branches and held us against the current.

Again the gobble rattled through the gray half-light. This was an old tom, the kind we were after. The power behind his gobble left no doubt about it. And he was not more than 50 yards downstream from the tangle of honeysuckle and briars we clung to. What a spot to get caught in. We were too close to the old swamp king to move in any direction. We had no choice but to get out then and there and try for an ambush.

We managed to get footholds on the muddy bank. A few minutes later Duff had his back against a tree, and I was in shooting position 10 yards further up the brushy slope. At the edge of what appeared to be a small clearing, I eased down behind a decayed log and waited for developments.

The hoot of an owl echoed from the river bottom far upstream. Immediately, the old gobbler challenged the owl with another booming gobble which sent new chills racing up and down my spine. The old tom was still on his roost, probably just out of gun range. At least, we hadn't spooked him.

Seconds ticked by, then minutes. Full dawn had crept in, but it was so foggy I could see only the dim outline of tall trees in the direction of the old gobbler's roost. Only the small clearing, not 20 yards long and 10 yards wide, would afford sufficient visibility for shooting.

Duff queried the old tom with a couple of short yelps. His second yelp was drowned out by a roaring gobble, then two others followed in rapid succession. This old tom was ready for company. I eased off the safety and stared into the foggy dawn.

In a few moments, Duff yelped softly again, and again the gobbler answered, but this time his challenge came from a point 20° further to my right. My heart almost stopped. The old bird had left his roost, and had glided down wide instead of flying in our direction. I surmised it was because Duff had yelped instead of clucking while the tom was still on his roost.

The light increased, but the fog thickened. For the next hour Duff and the old gobbler each played the same game. *"You* come to me!" Each time Duff yelped, the old gobbler would respond with a passionate gobble. The sound of the gobbles told us that he was prancing back and forth just out of sight in the thick fog. Then we heard the whirr of his wings as he tired of the game and flew to the opposite bank of the river. There, the old tom gobbled twice more, then was silent.

It was then that Duff and I discovered that the area fate had forced us to call from was a tiny island. To make matters worse, the island was completely covered with thick brush except for the one small clearing my stand overlooked. The tom could not have walked to us and no self-respecting gobbler would have flown to a call here.

Duff grinned. "Don't worry. That old bird wants company, and we'll kill him in the morning on the other side of the

Forest Service lands in both the Virginias and the Carolinas are inhabited by beauties like these which Duff Holbrook called up and photographed.

river." I wasn't sure of the certainty of that forecast, but I was sure of one fact which put high odds in our favor. Duff Holbrook knew South Carolina turkeys—and he was one of the finest turkey callers in the country. I was there to study this old pro in action as well as to check out float hunting tactics.

Duff, a wildlife biologist, is a Wildlife and Range Manager with the U.S. Forest Service in Atlanta. Previously, he spent many years living with and studying turkeys in the Santee River country in South Carolina's Francis Marion National Forest. During his many hours of observing this magnificent pure wild strain of birds, Duff learned their habits intimately —*and* how to converse with them.

This was several springs ago, and I had joined Duff for my first South Carolina gobbler hunt in Sumter National Forest—to be specific, that portion of the Forest just north of the town of Newberry. Only a few years before, the Sumter was almost completely barren of turkeys, but now it was loaded, thanks largely to Duff and capable biologists of South Carolina's Wildlife Marine and Resources Department who had trapped surplus turkeys from the Francis Marion and introduced them on the Sumter. Much of Sumter's wildest and most remote country lies along its many fast and winding streams. And I was already learning from Duff the tremendous advantages which accrue to the gobbler gunner sharp enough to float them.

The next morning we left my car at a bridge about three miles downstream from the old tom's roosting area, then hauled the kayak on Duff's car several miles upstream to the bridge where we had launched the previous morning.

The pre-dawn darkness was crisp, still, and fog-free, signalling a perfect morning for listening and for calling. Bright moon fire lighted our kayak path on the winding river and made navigation easy; that is, as easy as it can be in a kayak on a swift, log-jammed stream at night. As the fast water sang against steep banks, logs, and boulders, and as we glided by these threatening obstacles at an uncomfortable clip, I was mighty grateful that an expert like Duff was tailing the kayak.

In less than an hour, the wild ride was over and our ammunition was still dry. Duff eased the kayak into the mouth of a little branch about a quarter mile upstream from the area where Duff predicted the old gobbler would be roosting.

We reached the vicinity of the roost area, and Duff squatted down at the foot of a big pine and motioned me to join him. Our timing was perfect. The first trace of dawn was just beginning to silver the sky behind the thick pines. Duff cupped his hands around his mouth and hooted softly. Immediately he was answered by a thundering gobble, and it came from thick pines just over a slight rise ahead.

I went on point behind a big fallen log just ahead of Duff. When I last saw the old pro, he was easing his diaphragm call into his grinning mouth.

The next few minutes seemed like eternity. Neither Duff nor the old gobbler uttered a sound. I was positioned comfortably behind the log, well concealed and with an open view of our side of the rise. It was now getting light enough to see clearly. The crescendo of early morning birdsong faded, and at that moment Duff did cluck softly.

The stillness was shattered by a thundering gobble, then a second—and a third! I eased off the safety and lectured myself to be calm. The next time the gobbler sounded off, he was just over the rise from my stand, but as old hermit gobblers often do, he hung up there in spite of Duff's best rendered calls, which now were properly yelps. For the next hour, we could hear the old tom gobbling and strutting back and forth just out of sight on top of the rise. Each of Duff's yelps was perfect, but the wary old tom refused to budge. Then his gobbles told us he had moved across the rise and was circling left to a thick bottom behind us.

Duff eased over to me. "That sharp old cuss is call-shy. He heard my mouth caller too many times yesterday. But we'll creme him yet. I'll circle away from the bird, then up the hill and change calls on him. He'll either come to that— or he'll keep circling and come to yours."

The gobbler continued to sound off in the bottom and each gobble told me he was still circling left. I reversed my position behind the log and pulled out my box.

At that moment I heard a faint high-pitched yelp come from above me on the hill. Immediately that yelp was answered by the old tom and a minute later he gobbled again, this time from a point well to my *right*. The old tom was now heading directly for Duff—and at a dead run! I put my caller down.

A shotgun blast exploded. When Duff Holbrook fires once on a gobbler hunt, there is no doubt about results, so I headed for the source of the shot.

Duff was standing over one of the finest pure-blood Santee gobblers I have ever seen. Its long black and chestnut feathers, tinted with iridescent greens and golds, were sleek as satin. Its trim white crowned head was deep sky-blue. Its beard exceeded a foot in length. And its spurs were long, hooked, and razor-sharp. Duff lifted up his trophy for the supreme test. He hooked the old bird's spurs over a sturdy oak limb, and the magnificent bird hung there. When a man kills a pure-strain Santee gobbler which will hang by its spurs, he has accomplished the ultimate feat in turkey hunting. It was fitting that this supreme honor had gone to a man instrumental in introducing these birds in the area we hunted.

This exciting spring hunt illustrates several gobbler-hunting tricks worth emphasizing. First, float hunting can indeed skyrocket any hunter's odds for nailing a springtime tom. Much of the best turkey country throughout the East, like much of the Sumter, is laced by streams which can be floated, and most of these streams wind through rugged gobbler-loaded country which is difficult or impossible to penetrate by other means.

Float hunting enables the hunter to move swiftly and silently through prime gobbler country, thus maximizing his chances for hearing gobbles and thereby locating toms. And

Floating Eastern streams will often get the hunter into remote gobbler-loaded country. When you see or hear a gobbler, your hunt can begin—and you'll probably have no competition.

even if the hunter's first morning's crack at an old tom fails, it is a simple matter to pinpoint an area to hunt from the following morning, then to return there. And the float hunter doesn't have to hike long distances packing a load of hunting gear, or even pack out his gobbler. Best of all, when a gobbler is located in rugged remote country on a float hunt, it is highly unlikely that the hunter's try at the bird will be spoiled by another hunter.

Bridges cross most eastern streams at intervals rarely exceeding ten or twelve miles, a pleasant float of less than a day on most streams, even if the hunter pauses frequently along the stream to listen or to hunt. Sophistications such as boat ramps, however, are rarely available to the float hunter in eastern turkey country. Therefore, kayaks, canoes, or small aluminum boats are needed, and the lighter the better, for they may have to be carried long distances between the stream and auto. And a float hunt is, of course, a two-man and two-car operation—unless you have a patient and well-trained wife willing to sweat you out at the downstream bridge.

Novice floaters should have little difficulty executing a successful float hunt, provided they first float a strange stream during the daylight hours. Waiting for dawn to begin a fine float is not a tremendous handicap. Gobblers may be heard any time during the early hours. Even if they don't get a tom the first day, hunters can always load chow and a sleeping bag in the float boat, sleep near where they pinpoint tracks or hear gobbles, then work that area right at the crack of dawn the following morning. It makes sense, of course, to wear a life preserver during all floats, especially if the hunter is loaded down with cold weather clothing.

My trip with Duff Holbrook also sheds some interesting light on several aspects of calling spring gobblers. Duff has worked turkeys with every type of caller. Twenty years ago he mastered the wingbone, the leaf, the slate, and the box. Today, however, he works primarily with the diaphragm mouth caller or with his own voice. Duff's diaphragm caller, like those discussed in Chapter 2, is a small horseshoe-shaped metal disc with a center piece of thin rubber. He fits the caller against the roof of his mouth with the open end forward. And he blows from *deep* within his chest. Except for the gobble, Duff can duplicate any turkey call with amazing accuracy. He provides living proof that for those with a good musical ear, there is no better calling instrument for close range work.

Duff stresses that regardless of the caller he uses, the beginner should concentrate in the spring primarily on the two-to-six syllable yelp, just as recommended in Chapter 2. Duff believes that this one call has accounted for at least 90% of all spring gobblers ever called up and killed. Also, as previously indicated, Duff uses a coarse gobbler-like yelp and gets gobblers with it every spring. This again emphasizes that the rhythm of the call, is far more important than its tone.

The last trick Duff used to down that old Santee gobbler

Duff is an artist with his own mouth and diaphragm calls. Here he shows how to play deadly notes on the old wingbone, too.

also stresses the importance of being an opportunist. That old call-shy tom was finally lured in only after Duff changed his calling position and method of calling. Only a handful of experts can switch to voice calling, as Duff did, but anyone can change calling positions after an old gobbler hangs up and moves away from a call. Any new hunter can use different callers and sound like more than one turkey. One or both of these measures could well be just what it takes to lure in your next call-shy gobbler, too.

A few other suggestions may be of assistance to new float hunters or to those who are not yet experts with a call. If you're after a gobbler that will hang by his spurs, plan your float to cover the most inaccessible areas along the stream, for these are the areas most wise old toms hole up in. These usually are areas which your National Forest or county map indicates are furthest from roads.

If possible, plan to hunt at least a week. It should be stressed again that even during the spring mating season, gobblers will not sound off every day. Windy weather, in particular, can silence all or most gobblers anywhere. On the other hand, a sudden still morning is almost certain to make many gobblers along any stream sound off long and loud. Such a day is well worth waiting for.

When you hear a powerful loud and even gobble, as opposed to a puny broken one, the odds will be high that you've located a trophy tom. Beach the kayak or canoe, move to within good calling range, and use those calling tactics previously discussed.

If you don't nail the gobbler the first morning or hear another, listen where you heard that first one at dawn the next day. Call whether or not you hear him gobble, for the odds are high that the old tom will again be roosting in the same general area and within earshot of your call—and he may come without gobbling once.

Finally, the many gobbles I heard and the plentiful turkey sign I saw while floating the Sumter convinces me that this fine public hunting area is turkey-loaded. Maps, information on season dates and areas, and other required hunt-planning information may be obtained as follows: for hunting regula-

Floating at dawn put the author within earshot of this big gobbler. He called the bird in less than a hundred yards from where he left the boat.

tions, license and permit, contact South Carolina Wildlife and Marine Resources Department, P.O. Box 167, Columbia, 29211. For detailed Sumter National Forest map showing streams, roads, and campgrounds, contact Supervisor, National Forests in South Carolina, U.S. Forest Service, Columbia. For local information, contact District Ranger, U.S. Forest Service, or Wildlife Conservation Officer in Newberry 29108.

CHAPTER 5

Great New York And West Virginia Gobbler Hunts

It was midmorning. I got up and ambled back down the trail toward the car. And then I saw it—a big gobbler track etched in a patch of sand! I eased down by a boulder at the trail's edge. The track was probably old, but I would try calling once more.

I stroked the box four times in rapid succession, imitating the yelps of a lonesome hen. An immediate and nearby response shook me to the soles of my feet. I could hardly believe the gobble was real. Both Wayne Bailey and I had already worked this trail in the choice early hours without stirring up a single half-hearted answer. But this gobble *was* real. It came from the downhill side of the trail, from a stand of spruce and thick oak brush only two to three hundred yards ahead!

This gobble was not the fierce passionate rattle of a lovesick tom. It was a laconic gobble—the gobble of an old bird who had already serviced his hens and was trying to feed, but who suddenly found himself the unexpected target for further seduction.

This was a cool off-beat situation. The old bird had probably been engaged in lovemaking throughout the early morning—probably the reason why Wayne and I couldn't make him gobble earlier. Could I re-arouse him? Could I make him forget food and come to me at least for a look? I flattened myself against the boulder with my twelve ready on top of the rock. I waited five minutes and my blood quit boiling. Then I stroked the call gently, emitting three soft yelps.

After an eternity of two or three minutes, the old tom answered, still with a low gobble, but one which now said, "Here I am, gal—come closer and I'll look you over." At almost the same instant, I caught a flash of white gobbler head against the brushy wall of the trail. Then the entire body of the magnificent bird materialized. He was just out of gun range and I could only freeze—and sweat. The old gobbler looked as big as an elk and, as he stood in the open trail, the sun set fire to his imposingly beautiful and iridescent feathers.

Slowly and deliberately the wary bird crossed the trail and disappeared in the brush above it. At that moment I sensed movement behind me. I turned and nearly had heart failure. There, Wayne Bailey stood, squarely in the center of the open trail and not 50 yards below my position. I could only hope that the gobbler had not seen him. Somehow, my hunting partner had not seen the bird—or even heard his low gobbles! I motioned for Wayne to get down in the ditch at the trail's edge. He eased to my position and I briefed him in whispers.

Wayne pointed at himself, then toward the downhill side of the trail. I nodded in agreement and Wayne crawled back down and across the trail. If the old tom hadn't already seen my partner, his life expectancy was fast diminishing. Five minutes later, Wayne, who may be the country's leading artist with a box, yelped from 30 yards below my position. The gobbler answered almost immediately. He had not seen Wayne. Our deadly trap should work.

Certain that the strange hen was now working downhill away from him, the old tom rattled again, this time with real passion. Then he stepped back down in the trail and went into full strut. The barrel of my Remington 1100 with safety off, was already lined up straight at him. My eyes peered through a half-inch slot between my camouflaged cap brim and the gun barrel on the boulder. The boulder hid the rest of my body. I didn't move an eyelash. The gobbler strutted toward me, his breast feathers erect and his great drooping wings scraping the ground. The bird moved from 70 yards to 60, then to 50. In another few seconds the kill would be sure and I'd squeeze the trigger.

At that instant, a faraway shot rang out—and in a split second the gobbler went from full strut to full alert. He stepped fast to the downhill side of the trail. It was now or never. I squeezed off my charge of #4's. Feathers flew and the gobbler rolled to the ground. Then he fluttered into the air and managed to sail downhill. I was so surprised I didn't even get off a second shot. But there was no need. Wayne's twelve barked—and a few seconds later my partner emerged from the brush with the tom, a streamlined 19-pounder with a thick 9-inch beard.

This hunt took place a few Aprils back in the Allegheny Mountains near Marlinton, West Virginia, an area within an easy day's drive of many of the largest cities in the East. In fact, the day before the hunt I spent the night in Baltimore, then visited the next morning in Washington—and easily reached Marlinton by Jeep before dark. This was the first of two great gobbler hunts and trout trips I discovered that spring: trips which can be easily duplicated by most hunters living in the crowded East.

The Marlinton area is in the center of some of the wildest and most beautiful turkey and trout country I have ever seen. Until that trip, I didn't realize that there was so much game-loaded wilderness anywhere near crowded urban areas. Within a 40-mile radius of Marlinton, there are hundreds of thousands of acres of forested mountains and valleys. Much of it is accessible only by foot and it is all turkey range laced with trout streams. Best of all, most of this hardwood and pine-studded country is wide open to public hunting and fishing.

The best planning aid for a trip to this area is a Monongahela National Forest map. This map may be ordered from

If you don't score early, don't give up. Wayne Bailey nailed this beauty just a few minutes before the noon shooting deadline.

the Forest Supervisor, Monongahela National Forest, Elkins, West Virginia 26241. This map shows all 808,000 acres of the Monongahela in West Virginia and a vast adjoining area of the George Washington National Forest in both Virginia and West Virginia. Turkeys and trout abound over this entire vast domain of public lands where any man may hunt or fish.

Wayne Bailey, who is now North Carolina's top turkey biologist, hosted me during our West Virginia hunt at the state-owned Williams River Public Hunting Area just northeast of Marlinton. Camping facilities are meager here, but we heard gobblers from camp; I took many fine rainbows with spinners from nearby Williams River; and Wayne used his flyrod to fill our larder with fat bluegills from the camp lake.

Wayne is a native of Marlinton and was formerly a biologist and turkey management expert with the West Virginia Department of Natural Resources. In addition to the wild Gauley Mountain area where we ganged up on my West Virginia tom, Wayne recommends these additional areas for first class gobbler gunning:

1. The Cranberry back country
2. The Elk River area
3. Buckley Mountain
4. Allegheny Mountains along the West Virginia-Virginia border from Lake Sherwood Recreational Area north to Locust Springs Campground.

All the above areas are open to public hunting and can be easily pinpointed on a Monongahela National Forest map. This same map shows the location of campgrounds, many on or near trout streams. Gobblers range within hiking distance of all these campgrounds. Most gobblers are located, however, by hiking or driving ridgetops during the early hours and listening for gobbles at strategic points.

A big dividend in hunting from a camp along the crest of the Alleghenys is the fact that the taking of gobblers in each state is possible. Of course, to enjoy hunting on both sides of the border, you'll need a license from each state—*and* your hunt must be timed to coincide with spring gobbler seasons in both states. This magic date is usually in late April. For specific information on this spring's season dates, licenses and permit requirements, contact these agencies:

Department of Natural Resources, Charleston, West Virginia 25301;

Commission of Game and Inland Fisheries, P.O. Box 11104, Richmond, Virginia 23230.

And then on to New York—and another memorable gobbler hunt. From Marlinton, I steered north to southwestern New York's Allegany State Park, just south of Salamanca. And what turkey and trout country I found there—all of it within a day's drive of New York City, Buffalo, Philadelphia, Pittsburgh, and Cleveland. I was astounded. This beautiful public park, uncrowded at this time of the year, proved to be a game-loaded alpine wonderland.

My No. 1 hunting sidekick on this trip was Roy Orton, my rugged nephew from Ripley. I was giving Roy, who is now an old pro, his first taste of gobbler hunting. At the Park, Roy and I met my good friend and noted maker of Penns Woods Calls, Frank Piper. Frank is one of the nation's real experts with a mouth diaphragm. Each of us decided to go all out for the supreme thrill of hunting solo and calling up his own turkey.

It was May 4th. When the season opened at daylight, Roy and I had bulldozed the Jeep far up a remote hollow where we had located gobbler tracks the afternoon before. Roy was working the ridge on the left of the hollow and I was working the one on the right. Roy and I both heard gobblers that first morning but neither of us got close enough to work them. In the meantime, Frank Piper was busy becoming the first gobbler slayer that spring in Allegany State Park. Frank's revealing confession follows:

"I was late getting up and didn't make it to my chosen hunting area. I stopped my car at the first good ridge out of camp and called with my mouth caller—and at once a gobbler answered about three-quarters of a mile across a hollow and at the point of another ridge.

"Starting into the woods down over the side of the mountain, I heard the gobbler sound off once again. Crossing the bottom, I worked my way up the ridge on the same side as my prospective playmate. As I neared the top, I spotted an excellent hiding place in a burned out tree. I took a few minutes to complete arranging some dead branches and crawled in.

"I had every confidence that the bird would answer my yelps with a series of gobbles—but this didn't happen. I was then sure that my gobbler had crossed to the other side of the ridge. Getting out of my hiding spot, I topped the mountain and again situated myself in a recessed area on the forest floor. My position was excellent, *if* my bird came from the other side of the ridge. Calling again, I still didn't get a reply. But five minutes later, I heard leaves crack in back of me. Slowly turning my head, I saw what looked like two young gobblers. They must have seen me and worked downhill. A hen then flushed about four feet in the air and sailed down with them.

Then came the unbelievable sight of two old gobblers, tails in full fan and white heads bobbing directly toward me. A moment later, the birds turned and gradually worked away from me.

"Through all of this, there was still no gobble. Feeling as though I was completely surrounded by turkeys, I waited some ten to twelve minutes before correcting my position. Now in a better position and ready for action, I called again. Immediately both gobblers sounded off and the mountain shook. I called again, and stopped just in time to hear a hen yelping and coming directly to me. Frightened that she would see me and blow the whole show, I became extremely nervous. The hen worked around behind me, and produced calls that sounded better than mine. She moved to within five feet of me —and *still* didn't see me. Suddenly, off to the left the gobblers came—and beautifully within range! Happy was this lucky hunter as the bird I selected fell."

The next morning Roy Orton almost beat me to the second Allegany Park gobbler that season. Perched high on the same ridge where he had heard his gobbler the morning before, Roy began yelping with his new slate at daylight. And he did all right, especially considering that he had been introduced to this, his first turkey caller, only two days before. Roy called up a gobbler from a hollow a half-mile below his ridgetop perch. Unfortunately, the big bird circled and came in from above and behind, then spooked just out of range before Roy could shoot.

In the meantime, daylight found me climbing up the side of the opposite ridge proceeding to the area where I had heard gobbling the morning before. Suddenly, I thought I heard a distant gobble on top of the ridge. I continued to climb. In a few minutes, I could hear the gobbles clearly. They were coming from somewhere near the ridgetop, still a good quarter-mile above.

I could tell that this old tom was *really* ready. If I didn't get too close and spook him, he should be a set-up. I worked my way upward but well to the right of the gobbling. I wanted to be on or near the same contour as the old tom before I called. I proceeded as fast as possible until I approached within 100 yards of the ridgetop. There I paused until a booming gobble told me that the tom was just on the other side of the ridge and to my left. I eased to within 30 yards of the ridgetop and crawled behind the trunk of a big pine.

The pine trunk I faced gave me good concealment from the open ridgetop I expected my quarry to approach from. I laid my Remington on the ground along with my slate. I chalked my box and caught my breath. My position was ideal. The old tom couldn't see me until he topped the ridge ahead, and then he would be within easy range—*if* he came.

I pumped the box handle four times in rapid succession. The resulting yelps generated a booming reply: "GIL-OBBLE-OBBLE! GIL-OBBLE-OBBLE-OBBLE!" A minute later the woods rattled again and I could tell the old tom was working down the other side of the ridge toward me.

This is the box I used to call my old New York tom across the ridgetop. One series of yelps started him in my direction.

I put the box down, picked up the slate and scratched out a couple of low yelps—then reached for my gun. I knew the gobbler was coming in fast, but I didn't realize *how* fast. Before I even got my safety off, that big hunk of iridescent bronze topped the ridge at a dead run racing straight toward me. His radar eyes caught that part of me sticking out from the pine trunk—and he threw on the brakes, spewing a cloud of leaves into the air. I punched the safety and the old twelve went to my shoulder automatically. The gobbler instinctively cut to my left to get that pine trunk between me and him. I couldn't have had more than a six-inch swing—but somehow I made the grade.

I've killed many gobblers in many states, but this New York tom was one of the most beautiful. He was a 20-pound

The New York tom was one of the most beautifully colored birds I've ever taken. There's plenty more like him in Allegany State Park.

bird with richer chestnuts and more iridescent greens and golds than any tom I have ever taken. He was the second gobbler taken that spring in Allegany State Park.

Allegany State Park is almost sure to be open for gobbler gunning every spring. Spring gobbler season in the Park, as well as in most southwestern New York counties, is usually held in May. Hunting is permitted from daylight until late morning. In addition to a regular New York hunting license, a special wild turkey hunting permit is required to hunt gobblers anywhere in the state. These permits and other hunting and fishing information may be secured by writing the New York Conservation Department in Albany. An additional permit is required to hunt in Allegany State Park. These are available at the Park Police Hqs.

In addition to early morning turkey hunting, trout streams and lakes in the park are usually open and lightly fished during the early spring months. Nearly 400 individual cabins are provided in the park for public use. Most are intended as wilderness shelters and may not have cooking utensils, linens, or running water. However, bathhouses, wells and water hydrants are located near all cabins. Hotel lodge-type accommodations are also available, as are many beautiful campgrounds. All information on the Park and its facilities may be obtained by writing Allegany State Park Commission, Salamanca, New York.

The amazing comeback of the wild turkey in New York stems from several factors, one of the most important being the commendable emphasis placed on wild turkey management by able biologists and wildlife technicians of the New York Conservation Department. These experts tell me that gobbler gunning is just as good as in Allegany Park in *most* southwestern New York counties, including Cattaraugus, Chautauqua, Steuben, Tioga, Tomkins, Chemung, and Schuyler.

If there's finer gobbler hunting than in the areas I hunted in New York and the Virginias, I haven't found it—and I suspect that Wayne Bailey, Frank Piper, and Roy Orton will agree. So, I'm sure, will any reader who tries these great turkey areas once!

CHAPTER 6

How A New Tube Tricked An Old Kentucky Gobbler

There was no moon, but the faint outline of tall hardwoods against a skyful of twinkling stars guided me along the ridgetop. I stumbled over an occasional log, and brush and briars clawed at my thick trousers and snake-proof boots. I hurried, moving faster and faster for the knoll I *had* to occupy by the first crack of dawn.

When I reached the knoll, I collapsed on a decaying log and waited for my breathing and heartbeat to return to normal. The inky air was still—and cold—and touched by the subtle perfume of pine and dogwood blossoms. The deep silence about me was interrupted only by the soft monotonous notes of a lonesome whippoorwill telling its mate that spring had come.

I eased a #6 magnum into the barrel and followed it with two #2's. Then I felt for my box call to make sure it was in its proper place in my left pocket. The exhilerating wait for dawn and all its promise began. To this old gobbler hunter those golden pre-dawn moments alone make every spring turkey hunt worthwhile. As the new day is slowly born, great bronze gobblers, many of which you've seen many times before, go into full strut before your still unbelieving eyes and shatter the woods with their thundering gobbles—and you wait for a new tom, the biggest you've ever dueled, to challenge you at any second.

And this morning was no different from hundreds of other golden pre-dawn mornings in fine turkey woods from Wyoming and Colorado to New Mexico and Texas, and from Florida and Alabama to Virginia and New York. Yes, this morning was no different, except that it was unfolding in Kentucky's wild and beautiful Land Between the Lakes where I had never hunted gobblers before.

And dawn came in the same miraculous way. Beginning in the east, the Great Director snapped out the stars and replaced them with a sweep of slowly expanding grays and silvers. Hazy silhouettes turned into great oak, hickory, and maple trees wearing crowns of spring buds and tiny new leaves. The sky pinkened, and white dogwoods and green pines sprang out of the darkness. And a melody of birdsong began, then crescendoed to almost deafening proportions. That parade of old gobblers I had hunted before had long passed by. Now there was nothing but that big new gobbler roosting somewhere in a hollow below and new goose pimples racing up and down my spine.

The gobble rang out on schedule, well ahead of sunup, but it was not the loud booming gobble I had expected. Instead of roosting in a hollow close to the ridge I was on, as I had predicted he would the evening before, I could tell by the faintness of his rattle that the old bird was in a hollow to my right and several ridges over. My only course of action was to head straight for him with all possible speed. There was still a chance that I could reach his vicinity before he quit gobbling and before one of the other two hundred hunters who had checked into the area that morning beat me to him.

Twenty minutes and three steep ridges, later, I paused to get my breath and listen. I was in another ideal listening spot, on a long high ridge sparsely studded with ancient hardwoods holding up a sky now on fire with the first rays of the new sun. Before me, three small finger ridges jutted down into a deep and heavily timbered hollow. Across the hollow, on the side of the next high ridge, I could make out an old field covered with tall grass and tangles of briars and brush, a perfect magnet for nesting hens, and therefore, for gobblers, too.

"GIL-OBBLE-OBBLE-OBBLE! GIL-OBBLE-OBBLE-OBBLE!" The king of the forest was now announcing his supremacy from near the bottom of the brushy hollow ahead and directly down the finger ridge from my position. I eased down the side of the little ridge some two hundred yards and chose a calling spot behind the roots of a big oak upended by an old windstorm. My calling position could not have been more promising. I was completely shielded by the big mass of roots, yet I could see through them. And the country between my position and that of the love-crazed tom was almost barren of brush and trees—the kind of open terrain a wary old gobbler likes to use to approach a coy and stubborn hen.

I waited a few moments, placed my gun within easy reach and chalked my old box. Then I queried the tom with three soft yelps. He came back with a double gobble that shook me to the soles of my feet. He hadn't had a hen, and he was ready for one. But he was also cautious. Instead of running straight to me, like many toms will when they answer that first call with a double gobble, this wise old bird remained just out of sight in the hollow below. He gobbled again and again, coaxing me to come to him.

I played the waiting game for twenty minutes. Then I cradled the box in my hands to muffle my next series of yelps and to make the old tom think I was working away from him. Very softly I stroked out "Kee-oke, Kee-oke"—or "Good-bye, lover. It could have been great."

The old tom roared back with a passionate gobble. And then I saw him approaching in full strut. He was in no hurry. He moved slowly up the slope toward me, stopping every few minutes to strut and gobble. Through the tangle of roots, I watched him come. He closed to 100 yards, then 80. My safety had long been off, and I was watching him come over the barrel.

Suddenly, the old gobbler switched from full strut to a

posture of alarm. His long neck stretched high and he stood as still as a black stump. A second later he exploded into the air, topped the big hardwoods and sailed across the hollow toward the old field beyond. I heard the crunch of dry leaves on the main ridge above—and saw another hunter sneaking toward me.

When the young man, expertly camouflaged from head to toe, moved close to my position, I stood up and said "Hello." He put his finger to his lips, signaling me to be quiet, then tiptoed over. "There's a big gobbler gobbling just down there below!" he whispered.

I told the youngster what had happened. He apologized and we talked turkey for a few minutes, then parted. I used the rest of the morning to become familiar with the range of this big gobbler.

I focused my search in the vicinity of the long ridge with the old field across the hollow. I found a few hen and gobbler tracks in that area, and a couple of high knolls close to the field which would make promising listening spots for future hunts. I computed a compass course to this area from the nearest road on my map for future use, then another back to my car. I reached the check station a few minutes before the 11:00 checkout deadline.

The exciting sight of that big gobbler had already made my long trip from Florida to Kentucky's Land Between the Lakes worthwhile. I had left my outdoor writing tasks and had arrived for the six-day season on the afternoon before, April 14. This had given me a few pre-hunt hours to scout the woods, to find gobbler scratchings and tracks, and to select the listening point from which I had first heard the old gobbler on opening morning.

I made this trip to Kentucky for two primary reasons. I had long wanted to take a Land Between the Lakes gobbler because this was the only area where an original flock of our Kentucky turkeys, purportedly the largest of our eastern wild turkeys, exists today. According to Bob Smith, TVA biologist and turkey expert, this area has never been stocked with a transplanted bird, and the colony there is entirely pure, native blood. Second, I had already been lucky enough to take fairly easy gobblers in Florida and Alabama that spring, and I was looking for the challenge of a really difficult hunt. And no gobbler hunt in the U.S. is more difficult than that held each spring in Land Between the Lakes. About 200 hunters a day usually check in during each of the five or six day hunts, and they have rarely killed more than twelve gobblers during any one spring season.

Land Between the Lakes is one of the most scenic wild areas in the East. It is a 170,000 acre isthmus, completely uninhabited, magnificently wooded with mature forests and lying between Kentucky Lake and Lake Barkley, along the Kentucky-Tennessee border. It is managed by the TVA as a public recreational area, and abounds with whitetail and fallow deer, as well as harboring its modest but growing population

A close-up aerial shot of Land Between the Lakes, a beautiful area which every hunter should hunt at least once.

of wild turkeys of huge size. Eighty percent of the gobblers checked out during the last three spring hunts weighed between 21 and 24 pounds!

Kentucky Dam Village State Park, near the little town of Gilbertsville, is less than a thirty minute drive from Land Between the Lakes north entrance check station. For this reason, I had made arrangements to bunk in a cabin there during my gobbler hunt. I returned to the cabin, grabbed lunch and an hour's sleep, left my gun, then headed back for a more thorough study of the hunting area.

I decided to scout new territory with the hope of finding more sign and an alternate hunting spot. On a dim road crossing a remote hollow, I had the good fortune to run into two other wild-eyed gobbler chasers, who have since become my very close friends. Harold Knight, who owns a barbershop in Cadiz, Kentucky, and Dave‑Hale, a farmer from nearby Gracey, were intimately familiar with every inch of turkey range in Land Between the Lakes. Both had taken big gobblers during two of the last four spring hunts. These congenial young natives appraised me for a few minutes, then took me in like a long lost friend. They briefed me on the most promising areas to scout—then showed me my first tube turkey caller.

Harold Knight's new tube was radically different from any caller I had previously seen, and I fell in love with its realistic hen yelps at once. I conned Harold out of one of his plastic or "Pill Bottle" calls, and fortunately from that point till this day I staked most of my gobbler hunting success on its remarkable effectiveness.

When we separated that afternoon, Harold and Dave had circled several areas with turkeys on my Land Between the Lakes map which I had obtained along with my hunt permit by writing the TVA Information Office at Golden Pond, Kentucky. We were all independent turkey hunters, and agreed to scout and hunt separately but to meet at the check station to compare notes after each morning's hunt.

I spent the remainder of the afternoon hiking through turkey country Harold and Dave had marked on my map. I found scattered old tracks and scratching, but no sign indicating a concentration of birds. I listened on a promising knoll from sunset to dark, but wasn't lucky enough to hear a gobble or a bird fly up to roost.

For the second morning, my alarm buzzed at 2:30. By 3:30, I had polished off a quick breakfast and had reported at the check station. When it began to get light a little after 4 a.m., I was on the same finger ridge where I had last seen the old tom the previous morning. Again, it was quiet, still, and cold, a perfect morning for gobbling. But not a bird sounded off in my area. I called from many likely spots through the rest of the morning, but got no results. I was back scouting more new territory by midafternoon and remained until black dark, but failed to hear a bird or find significant sign.

The third day was a disappointing duplication of the second, except that I worked the ridges and hollows around the old field, and discovered enough fresh sign to convince me that hens were indeed nesting in the old field, and that at least one old gobbler, probably the one I had worked the first day, was still using the area. Harold and Dave had heard gobblers both days but had also failed to score.

The last three days of the hunt didn't begin until April 22, giving me four days of needed rest—and the chance to wrestle with Kentucky Lake's slab-sided crappies. I fished with Dick Douglas and Bill Jones out of Cedar Knob Resort, Benton, Kentucky, and had a great time. I heartily recommend this bonus fishing fun to any turkey hunter who visits Land Between the Lakes.

On April 22, torrents of rain poured down during the entire day. All morning I shivered under a pine on one of the knolls near the old field, hoping that the rain would stop, but I was rewarded only with a bad cold. The next morning, however, was another perfect gobbling morning: clear, crisp, and still.

Well before dawn, I was perched on a comfortable stump in the center of a fallen treetop. I was on a high knoll adjacent to the old field which I knew birds were using. From my well-shielded position, I could hear any gobble which might come from either of the two big hollows on both sides of the field, and I knew when light came my gun would command the only open clearing in the area, one between the thick grass and brush in the field and the thick forest which bordered it. I knew that this little clearing was a likely fly-down spot for any gobbler which might be roosting near it, and a likely strutting spot for any gobbler in that general area. This hunting area was also promising because it was two miles from the nearest road; therefore, competition from other hunters would be unlikely.

That familiar parade of old gobblers passed by. Light and birdsong finally came—and I waited for that booming gobble which I fully expected to hear at any moment. Just before sun-up, a dim and distant gobble echoed far to the north. But I remained in my comfortable hiding spot, knowing there had to be at least one good gobbler in my immediate vicinity.

The new sun now blazed through the big hardwoods—and still no sound from my gobbler. I decided to make the first advance. Cupping Harold Knight's magic tube in my hands, I queried the forest with a series of four soft inquisitive yelps. But only a distant crow answered. I remained in my strategic position for another fifteen minutes, then yelped again. I couldn't help marvel at the realism of the mellow notes this new call produced. If there was indeed a gobbler around, he should already be in the treetop with me.

Another fifteen minutes passed and I had almost given up. If there was a tom in the area, I decided that he already had a harem of hens or had been spooked off his roost by some other wandering hunter in one of the bottoms below.

It was then that I made the most unforgivable mistake a gobbler caller can make. I left my gun on the ground and stood up to stretch. The forest exploded behind me. The crash of breaking limbs was almost deafening. Instead of picking up my gun, I turned to watch the big buck, causing this noisy disturbance, leap away. But the buck was a monster gobbler propelling his great body straight up through the tangle of brush and trees! I stood there hypnotized, with a foot-long beard inching upwards not ten yards from my face. The vertical speed of the great bronze blur slowly increased, like a big rocket leaving the launch pad. Even when the big tom leveled off above the treetops, he would still have been an easy shot— *if* I had had my gun!

I sat back down on the stump and the full impact of my

monstrous misfortune gradually permeated my shocked brain. I had called the sneaky old tom to within a few yards of my position. If he had gobbled one time he would have been easy prey. If I had waited a few seconds longer before standing, I would have seen him. If I had observed the fundamental precaution of picking up my gun before I stood up, he would have been a sure target. Even if I had picked up my gun when I heard the explosion behind me, I still could have killed him. I concluded that Someone Up There just didn't want me to kill a Land Between the Lakes gobbler. But I *knew* the new tube call had worked.

That afternoon, I joined in one last critique and strategy session with Harold and Dave. Both these turkey pros smiled knowingly when I told them about muffing my big opportunity. "None of us turkey chasers will ever get good enough not to be whipped by wary old gobblers," Harold consoled. "And that's exactly the reason we keep right on chasing them."

The next morning would be it. Either we would score then, or go home empty-handed. Dave had located an old bird which gobbled its head off that morning. It came to his call, but hung up just out of gun range over a ridge. Dave didn't think he had spooked the old tom—and that was the bird he intended to make his last gamble on.

Harold had located a remote hollow that morning where three birds were gobbling at daylight. He thought he had called one of them up well after sunup, but the bird approached in thick brush and he couldn't positively identify it as a gobbler, and, of course, he let it go. Harold was certain that none of these old toms had been spooked, and he encouraged me to try for one of them the next morning. We got out our maps and Harold laid out two courses from the nearest road to the two main ridgetops on each side of the hollow. Harold selected the ridgetop that he would occupy at dawn, and strongly recommended that I head for the other. Since I had spooked the old tom out of my favorite area that morning, Harold's plan seemed to make a lot of sense. I told him that I would probably be there.

For the first night of my long hunt, I hit the sack feeling completely defeated. I had only one morning left to outwit a wary gobbler on the toughest ground I had ever dueled on. I had only two last dawn listening points to choose from, and neither was very promising. If I went to the area Harold had suggested, I would be severely handicapped by not being familiar with the terrain. If I went to my old listening post, the old gobbler I had spooked the morning before would probably be roosting a mile away. Once more, I set the alarm at 2:30 and passed out.

By the time I left the check station that final morning, it was almost four o'clock. I decided to gamble on the new ridge Harold has suggested and headed for our pre-selected parking area. About halfway there, I passed the familiar jeep trail that led toward my old hunting spot. I couldn't keep my foot from slamming down on the brake pedal. I pulled into the trail, then started to back out again. After all, I had decided that Harold's new spot would offer me the greatest promise. But a Voice inside me commanded, "Go down your old trail." And I did. I parked the Bronco in the same old spot and made the same long pre-dawn journey to my stump in the fallen treetop overlooking the small clearing. Only this time, I was ten minutes later than usual, and dawn came so quickly there was no time to watch that parade of old gobblers go by in the dying darkness. And I sat on the stump almost without hope, and thinking only of how I had spooked the big gobbler from this very spot the morning before.

One last time, I watched the magic of a Kentucky forest slowly materialize. It was another crisp silver dawn and the eastern sky was streaked with pink now. A mighty gobble rang out, so near me that I could hardly believe it was real! The old tom was roosting in neither the hollow to my right, nor to my left. He was roosting on a steep ridge side not 200 yards below the little clearing my gun commanded.

No turkey hunter deserved a second golden opportunity like this—but it was real—and it was mine. I eased the little tube to my lips and cupped it tightly in my hands. Somehow, I managed to emit a reasonable facsimile of three very soft and sleepy clucks. A few seconds later, I heard the churning of great wings. And the big gobbler sailed down directly in the center of the little clearing before me. My gun was on him when he landed, and from that moment on he was mine. From my well-hidden position, I watched him ruffle his mass of multi-colored feathers, and stretch one big wing. His thick beard almost dragged the ground. Then his sky-blue head raised high as he stretched his long warty neck. His beady eyes burned straight into mine, and I fired holding a few inches high.

The old monster crumbled as the charge of #6's slapped his head and upper neck. Slowly, I walked over to him and absorbed the full magnificence of the moment. It was not yet sunup, yet another of hunting's greatest moments had already unfolded in the splendor of those wild Kentucky hills. I

Harold Knight (left) admires my 22-pound Land Between the Lakes gobbler, the biggest gobbler I've ever bagged.

carried my trophy to the nearest limb and the beautiful bird hung from it by his long sharp spurs! How I wished that Duff Holbrook, Wayne Bailey, and Frank Piper, and that other host of dedicated turkey hunters I have been privileged to know over the years could have shared this supreme moment with me. But I *could* share it with Harold Knight and Dave Hale.

Harold Knight demonstrates the deadly tube call which gave me my Land Between the Lakes gobbler, and which he invented. Since that time, I have taken most of my spring gobblers with Harold's tube.

I flung the big bird over my shoulder and headed for the Bronco and check station.

Harold and Dave had not scored, but they were as exuberant at my good fortune as I was. On the check station scales, my old tom weighed 22½ pounds—making him the heaviest Eastern gobbler I have ever killed. His thick beard measured 10 inches even. He was one of eight toms killed that spring in Land Between the Lakes.

When I headed back to Florida, I said goodbye to Harold and Dave and remarked one more time, "This was one of my greatest gobbler hunts—I don't know how I could have been so lucky!" Dave was kind enough to reply, "It wasn't all luck. You worked harder than any of the rest of us, and remember it was that new tube of Harold's that lured the old bird in." And Harold Knight's amazing tube has continued to lure gobblers in for me ever since.

If you would like to duplicate this great Kentucky gobbler hunt, you may obtain permits and complete hunt information by writing:

Director of Information
Land Between the Lakes
Tennessee Valley Authority
Golden Pond, Kentucky 42231

CHAPTER 7

Mixing Wild Gobblers
And Brawny Bass

Clark Hill Reservoir is one of the finest spring bass hotspots in the South—and big gobblers roam both its Georgia and South Carolina banks. There, gobbler seasons are open through most of April when bass are hitting best. These factors make this twisting ribbon of silver and its surrounding Piedmont hills a perfect springtime destination for those who thirst for both bass action and gobbler thunder.

My last South Carolina gobbler hunt was unforgettable. It began in late April with a strange and prolonged duel with another beautiful transplanted gobbler—this time between Little River Sportsman's Camp on Clark Hill Reservoir and the turkey-hunting town of Edgefield. Vernon Bevill, one of the Wildlife and Marine Resources Department's top young biologists, introduced me to this old gobbler. Our craggy hilltop listening point was still bathed in yellow pre-dawn moonlight as we uncased our guns and began listening for gobbler music.

The sky began to silver and two gobblers sounded off almost simultaneously. Vernon headed for one bird which was

Wild gobblers and brawny bass abound on both the Georgia and South Carolina banks of Clark Hill Reservoir.

gobbling in a hollow just north of the pine-fringed hilltop. Mine was thundering from a creek bottom a half-mile to the south. I started down the still dark hillside with all possible speed aiming for a calling point well to the left of the old gobbler's roosting spot. After kicking my way through tangles of briars and brush, and penetrating a rough course of scrub oak and pine, finally I reached a fairly open hardwood slope some 200 yards above the old tom's position.

I eased down behind a log with my back against a large

pine, removed the muffling cloth between the lid and sound chamber of my old box, and sent two sleepy "Clucks" in the tom's direction. The gobbler responded with a passionate double gobble and I knew he would fly down from his roost in my direction. I placed the box on the ground, then eased my new tube caller, which I now had complete confidence in, from my pocket and waited.

The sky reddened and the top half of the new sun emerged in the pines on the hilltop across the creek. At that moment, the old tom's almost continual gobbling ceased for several minutes. His next gobble was low and muffled and I knew he had flown down. Cupping the little tube in my hands, I teased him with one run of four soft hen yelps—then picked up my gun, punched the safety off—and froze.

The old tom's next series of gobbles told me that he had run straight uphill toward me and was now strutting just below a steep bank less than 100 yards below. For fifteen minutes, the gobbler sounded off from that same strutting spot, trying his best to get me to come to him, as any cooperative hen should. Then abruptly, he quit gobbling. The woods grew dead quiet. My old twelve got heavier and heavier and sweat began rolling down my forehead.

The almost unbearable suspense continued. Suddenly, I heard a twig crack behind me and to my left, and out of the corner of my eye, I saw the bronze statue of a turkey, half concealed by brush, standing less than 10 yards away! I was nearly 100% sure that this was the old tom that had circled and come in behind me. But patches of brush and the poor light made it impossible for me to see either his head or breast clearly. Knowing the bird might be a stray hen, I waited. Suddenly, there was a loud "Putt!" and the air was filled with exploding wings. Only when the rising bird turned half toward me in a patch of brilliant sunlight could I see its long beard and blue head. The range was questionable, so I lowered my gun and watched the old tom fly across the creek and disappear in the pines beyond.

I returned to our hilltop listening point and met Vernon an hour later. He had also worked his tom, but the bird had spooked just out of gun range. Vernon announced that he would be unable to hunt with me for the next couple of days. He suggested that I head for a new area the next morning rather than try to work the toms we had already spooked. But I have never been able to break off a duel with an old gobbler that easy. So I told Vernon I would hunt the same area the next morning, too.

Again, my gobbler sounded off at first light, but this time he was roosting much further away and high on the hillside he had spooked to the morning before. By the time I reached his general vicinity, the sun was already up and he had flown down from his roost. I worked toward the gobbling, but was stopped by a large clearing with no cover whatsoever. The old tom had set up a strutting area on a ridgetop beyond and was gobbling his head off.

I was afraid to cross the clearing as the old tom might spot me—and I was afraid he would quit gobbling before I could go around it. My best option appeared to be to attempt calling him across the 200-yard opening, even though I knew it would be difficult. The gobbler was too far away to hear my tube, so I gave him a loud run of snappy yelps on the box. He gobbled back immediately, but several succeeding gobbles told me he was sticking to the same strutting area, waiting for me to come to him. I gave the old bird two more series of yelps at ten minute intervals but he continued to hang up.

The sun was now well above the pines and was rapidly heating up the woods. I knew my chance for scoring was growing short. For a long period all gobbling ceased but I remained in my oak-clump hiding spot on the clearing edge hoping against hope that the old tom might still come. A few minutes later, I saw black movement in a fringe of pines on the far side of the clearing.

The tom was still 200 yards away. Now I knew my only hope was in my tube. I placed its diaphragm against my lower lip and threw him two soft and seductive yelps. He stepped into the green clearing and went into full strut. His jet black feathers glistened like onyx in the sunlight. He broke the strut, let go with one thundering gobble—then began *running* straight for me with his head stretched out just above the ground. I had never before had a gobbler approach me so long in view and in such a speedy fashion. I raised my 1100 to my shoulder and held it on the racing black blur. The gobbler reached 50 yards, then 40, then 30—and I waited and waited for him to stop and for his head to come up. But he didn't stop and erect his warty periscope until he was almost in the oak clump with me. For the microsecond that I looked at him over my gun barrel at a scant 10 yards range, I'd swear that I saw his head turn from blue to red. As I squeezed the trigger, he crouched to flush and his alert head snapped down. I thought I had missed the gobbler at point-blank range. I jumped to my feet to swing again on the sky-reaching mass of black, but the old tom collapsed in midair before I could get off the second shot. I walked up to the crumbled monarch and saw a tiny spot of red on his white leathery crown. A single #6 from the lower part of the pattern had done the job. He weighed an even 17 pounds and had a 10-inch beard.

Spring had also charged Clark Hill's largemouths into a high

Relaxing with my South Carolina gobbler and a five-pound bass. I got them both on the same day while working out of Little River Sportsmen's Camp.

state of activity. They had left the deep water and were swarming in the shallows. Almost every rocky point and brushy cove within two miles of my cabin at Little River Sportsmen's Camp produced bass, and I exercised scores of them. Most of the largemouths were in the one-to-three-pound category, but I took a few four-and five-pounders. All the lunkers and most of the yearlings went for a purple worm fished weedless and with a small split shot positioned a foot above the #1-0 hook.

I also discovered that Clark Hill has a good population of white bass and white-striped bass hybrids, some of which I also exercised. More important, as I fished during the early and late hours, I heard more spine-tingling gobbler music on both the Georgia and South Carolina banks!

Two days later, the Georgia turkey season opened on Clark Hill Management Area, a few miles downstream from the Little River Camp. There, biologist J. Dan Marshall, one of Georgia's top turkey experts who worked out of the Management Area Headquarters, gave me a map and briefed me on hunting hot spots. For three days, I tried closing on those wild Georgia gobblers by boat, but the sound of my motor turned them off. I switched to my Jeep and drove to high listening points in the Management Area for two more days, but failed to hear a gobbler.

On the sixth day of my Georgia hunt, Dan Marshall, who had already taken his gobbler a few days before, escorted me to a high ridge, then headed on down the road to listen from another spot. The sky was just graying as the rear of his truck vanished from view. A moment later, a faint gobble echoed from a dark hollow nearly a mile below. I've covered a lot of hellacious country to close on gobblers, but none matched the ruggedness of this penetration.

The first half mile was a dark hectic descent through tangles of honeysuckle, and across steep gully walls, windfalls, and piles of big pine limbs left from old logging operations. Then I had to cross at least a quarter mile of swamps and wade two knee-deep creeks—all before good daylight.

But I was lured continuously on by some of the deepest and coarsest gobbling I had ever heard. As I approached reasonable calling range, a third creek loomed before me in the half-light. It was about 20 feet wide and its depth was impossible to judge. But attempting to call the old gobbler across that wide stretch of water was a task I knew better than to undertake. So I removed my wallet and shells from my pockets, loaded my gun, and tied my calls to my gun barrel.

I was able to wade the creek with my head and gun just above the water. Shivering from both the cold water and that hot gobbler music, I climbed the opposite muddy bank and beheld a perfect calling spot. Not three feet from the creek bank, a waist-high wall of honeysuckle offered perfect concealment—and in front of the honeysuckle the creek bottom opened up like an oversized theater stage. Only a few big and widely spaced hardwoods obstructed my view of the clearing. This opening would make a perfect approach route for the old gobbler still sounding off from his roost tree some 200 yards beyond.

I knelt down behind the honeysuckle so that only my eyes and head protruded above the green wall. I untied the calls from my gun barrel, removed the muffling cloth from the box, and let the old tom have two low and widely spaced "Clucks." He answered with two of the most ferocious double-gobbles I've ever heard. Then, a few minutes later, I heard him fly down from his roost. After an eternity of quietness, which probably lasted not more than five minutes, he gobbled again —this time just beyond the clearing I surveyed.

I forced myself to wait, which I knew teased the old gobbler unmercifully. After some five minutes more, I picked up my trusty little tube and administered the *coup de grace:* that same series of soft and seductive hen yelps that had just done in the South Carolina gobbler.

My gun was in my hands and the safety off when the old monarch appeared on that stage of emerald grass just touched by the new sun. There, for a full thirty minutes, I watched the greatest performance a man can behold in all the great outdoors. With chestnut tail spread wide, and with long beard and great wings scraping the ground, the old king pranced back and forth in front of me in full strut. As he strutted, his leathery cheeks were violet blue. His white crowned head was arced low in a jet black mass of erected neck and breast feathers. "Vtt-

Veroomi!" came the sound of his booming strut. Periodically his long neck would shoot straight out, and his head would change to fiery red and shake out a violent "GIL-OBBLE! GIL-OBBLE-OBBLE-OBBLE!" At frequent intervals, the old monarch would drop his strut and stand like an inky statue with his warty neck stretched high and with his beady eyes burning straight into that patch of honeysuckle I was hiding behind. He was getting impatient. He wanted that hen to come out.

Admiring him for so long, I felt an unusual amount of reverence for this majestic old bird—but I told myself that he had already serviced every hen in his area and was probably too old to survive another winter. More to the point, he ap-

I had to wade three creeks to get to my big Georgia gobbler, but the trophy was worth the effort. Again, it was a cluck on a box while he was still on his roost, then a run of sweet tube music that did him in.

peared to be one of the finest trophies I had ever had the chance to take—and I had earned him.

Again in full strut, he moved behind the trunk of a big hardwood. The moment his head disappeared behind the tree, I eased the twelve to my shoulder. I saw the tail close and drop straight down and knew he had caught my movement. My cagy quarry refused to budge from his shielded position—and I knew better than to move from mine. Finally, the old gobbler raced for cover and I managed to swing successfully on his long outstretched neck. My reward was a 12-inch beard and a magnificent pair of jet black spurs more than an inch long. These, plus the majestic tail fan of this old 19-pound Clark Hill gobbler, will always occupy a place of high honor on my den wall.

The story of the return of wild gobblers to both the Georgia and South Carolina banks of Clark Hill is the same exciting one told in Chapter 4—and a real tribute to the Georgia Game and Fish Commission as well as to the South Carolina Wildlife Service; all these agencies contributed to the effective turkey restocking and management program in this area. Result: today wild turkeys abound where there were none a few short years ago. And bright dedicated young biologists, like Vernon Bevill and Dan Marshall, are carrying on this important work.

Dan Marshall was as thrilled with my trophy as I was. We celebrated over a quick cup of coffee, then spent the rest of the day further testing the fettle of those plentiful and fighting Clark Hill bass, which we again found concentrated on the points and in the coves. And again, purple worms racked up the most bass, but a yellow spin beetle with soft plastic body produced almost as well.

As we headed back to the dock with the dying sun dancing on our wake, Dan mused, "I'll bet you don't know many places where you can take fine gobblers in two states and catch easy limits of bass—all within a few miles of your cabin door." There are other spots in Dixie where this can be done in March or April, but none of them that I know of offers a higher promise of both bass and gobbler action than Clark Hill Reservoir. If you decide to head that way to quench your springtime bass and gobbler thirst, contact these agencies for hunting and fishing information:

Georgia Game and Fish Commission Office
Thomson, Georgia 30824
South Carolina Wildlife and Marine Resources Department
Edgefield, South Carolina 29824

Or, contact: Little River Sportsmen's Camp
Route 1
Appling, Georgia 30802

CHAPTER 8

A Classic Virginia Gobbler Hunt

It was whipped from under a wing. Its blue lid snapped open. Its coal black pupil contractel slightly in its moist sphere of brown. In a microsecond, its sharp lens focused from warty head to infinity. And it scanned the brightening horizon still yellow with moonlight in the direction of the owl hoot.

It read the flicker of a cardinal's tail in a distant oak . . . then the race of a mouse across a log under the roost tree. It searched the remainder of the brushy hollow below, inch by inch, and studied every foot of adjacent hardwood ridges. As daylight came, it swept the brown forest floor with increasing microscopic intensity, and finally signalled the brain that all was well.

Now it dropped low in a black mass of erecting breast feathers set against a chestnut tail fanned wide. Its lid half closed. It was almost lost in a swelling leathery head of ever changing blues, whites, and reds. An instant later, the lid re-opened—and glazed with passion, it was propelled straight out from the breast and the roost limb, a shining blur on the end of a violently shaking bill-tipped shaft. "GIL-OBBLE-OBBLE-OBBLE! GIL-OBBLE-OBBLE-OBBLE!"

The eye of the gobbler, ten times as powerful as man's, had done its first job in the critical early morning minutes of spring.

I felt the mountaintop shake as this old tom thundered his delayed challenge to my owl hoot. I could tell that he was roosting on the still-dark west side of the mountain not more than 300 yards below. A few minutes later, two other toms started rattling off in rapid-fire unison far down the mountain to the south.

A red sun set the cloud-pimpled sky on fire, and I surveyed the vast northern Virginia wilderness below. In every direction from my lofty throne, rocky hardwood ridges and hollows dropped sharply down to distant stream bottoms, most heavily wooded, but a few cleared and green. Across this brown expanse of ideal turkey range, white dogwoods paraded and patches of redbuds outflamed the new sun.

By now, all three old toms were gobbling with mad fury, and a fourth young bird, a half mile below the nearest old tom, was trying his squeaky best to sound like a monarch, too. I made mental notes of the roosting spots of the nearest old tom and the young bird. The distant gobblers were roosting together fairly close to the cabin that would serve as our hunt headquarters. So, I began the hectic thirty minute jeep descent to that spot. Once more, a pre-dawn recon trip to the highest listening point in a spring turkey hunting area had paid off.

After reaching the cabin, I walked to the first ridgetop to the north. The two toms I had heard from the distant mountain were still gobbling. They were moving slowly up the ridge just across a small creek immediately below me. One look at a dense stand of timber in the creek bottom to my right told me this was the exact spot where these birds had roosted—and the exact spot where they would probably roost that night too, if they weren't disturbed.

How could a turkey "guide" get so lucky! If I ever needed a promising starting point for a spring hunt, it was that precise moment, for the next morning I wanted to show a real gobbler hunt to two of my best friends: Lamar Underwood, *Sports Afield's* distinguished editor, and the same indomitable Frank

Piper, call manufacturer and caller supreme, who had hunted with me in New York's Allegany State Park the year before.

Lamar showed up that night eager for combat the next morning with his first springtime tom, an experience he had somehow missed while chasing everything else that swims, flies, or runs. He was accompanied by Hans Carroll, *Sports Afield's* staff photographer with the mission of recording on honest Ektachrome the success or failure of our cagy campaign. A little later Frank Piper arrived. We had only two thin mornings to cut the mustard.

Before sacking out, Frank and I spent an hour designing battle plans, tuning calls and briefing Lamar and Hans on their tactical assignments. Frank and Lamar would attack the two gobblers just below camp, with Frank calling and Lamar on point with his trusty twelve some 20 yards ahead. It was difficult for Frank to accept the unique fact that someone else had actually roosted two gobblers for him within easy hiking distance of camp. So, I walked him to the ridge in the golden light of a near-full moon and pointed out the roosting area in the creek below. And so help me, at that moment one of the gobblers actually sounded off in the moonlight—and right where he was supposed to be!

Frank had worked over so many gobblers, that he had supreme confidence that he could call the old toms up the same ridge we were standing on, even though I told him their movement pattern the morning before was up the ridge on the opposite side of the creek. This was his ball game, so I helped him build hasty blinds for himself and his dead-eye partner at points of his selection. My plan was to attack the old sharp-eyed bird on the distant mountaintop at first light, then to return for Hans later. We agreed to leave the cabin a full hour before daylight, so that there would be no chance that the sound of my Jeep would spook Frank's and Lamar's birds.

On the back of my truck was an amazing new backwoods camper developed by Skamper. It had been my home that spring through nearly two months of spring gobbler chasing from Florida, through Georgia and the Carolinas, then up through Virginia. The top popped down for low-profile, enabling me to penetrate most wild turkey country with camper.

And when I hit really hellacious 4-wheel-drive-only country, a set of built-in jacks made instant removal of the camper possible. With this combination, I always had go-anywhere off-roads mobility plus comfortable living quarters never far away. I passed up a strange bunk in the cabin for my familiar camper bed, and set the alarm for 3:30.

An owl hooted—a whippoorwill sounded off—my gobbler answered, and good daylight was still fifteen minutes away. To eliminate any chance of spooking the gobbler, I had left the Jeep far below the moonlit mountaintop and was inching my way down to the last ridge separating me from the hollow I knew the old tom was roosting in. I moved to a shallow indentation on the ridgetop about 200 yards above the bird. This was an ideal calling position, since, as previously indicated, old mountain gobblers are easiest to call uphill, and since the terrain would make it impossible for him to see me until he topped the ridge in sure range. What a setup! I was sure to be back in camp by 8 a.m. with a long beard for Hans to photograph.

The old tom rattled once more before good light, then began gobbling in earnest. Every time a crow cawed or a squirrel barked, he thundered back a challenging reply. For ten more minutes, he gobbled continuously, and I let him sweat. Then, with my old box, I gave him a couple of muffled tree clucks, just loud enough to let him know that another turkey was roosting in my vicinity. After he hit the ground, I would give him one sexy run of hen yelps on my tube, then pick up my gun.

The volume of the gobbles suddenly diminished, and I knew the bird was on the ground. After a short pause, I gave him that irresistible dose of tube music. He thundered back a passionate double gobble. Then there was dead silence. I picked up my gun and goose pimples raced up and down my spine. I *knew* he was on his way. At that moment three shots rang out just below the ridgetop, and I saw the old tom, with wings set, gliding toward a distant bottom below. I looked over the ridgetop and saw another hunter racing downhill after the spooked tom.

We were hunting on private land where I hadn't anticipated hunter interference, but we were close to turkey-loaded George

Washington National Forest, and the hunter had probably
crossed over from there. This was difficult to understand, because I had heard so many gobblers while scouting the George
Washington two mornings before, that we had almost de-
clined our invitation to hunt on this ranch in order to hunt
there. Turkey hunting is equally good on Virginia's Jefferson
National Forest to the southwest. In fact, thanks to intensive
wildlife management cooperation between the Forest Service
and Virginia's Division of Game and Inland Fisheries, there
may be more turkeys on these two forests than on any other
area of comparable size in the East, and both are open for
both spring and fall turkey hunting. You can get maps and
full information on both these forests by writing: Southern
Region Hqs., U.S. Forest Service, 50 Seventh Street, N.E.,
Atlanta, Georgia or by contacting the Forest Supervisor or the
District Ranger when you arrive in either Forest.

I headed back to the cabin, but failed to hear another bird.
No gobbler hung in the tree in front of the cabin—but the
instant I spotted that wild tell-tale gleam in Lamar's eyes, I
knew he had been given a full charge of gobbler tonic. "It was
just great! It was *just* great!" he kept mumbling over and over
again, while Hans Carrol smiled.

Frank Piper was less exuberant. "Those two gobblers
answered my *every* call—and gobbled their heads off for an
hour. But I just couldn't get them to cross that creek and come
up our ridge. It was a beautiful morning anyway!"

"I still think it's better to try the ridge *across* the creek
in the morning," I suggested. "There just aren't many gobblers
that can be called across a creek."

Frank was forced to agree. "I hate to admit I have to do
it the easy way, but that's just where we'll be in the morning."

"Y-e-a-h!" Lamar chimed in. "We'll get 'em in the morning! You ought to hear Frank call. With that mouth diaphragm, he sounds more like a turkey than a turkey. Every
time he called, both those gobblers roared back like they
couldn't stand it. I thought they'd cross that creek and stomp
us to death. It was *just* great!"

Hans Carrol had only heard the early morning racket from
the cabin yard, but he was already hypnotized by gobbler

music, too. The reason he was only grinning was because his mouth was full of one of Frank's diaphragm callers and he was busy working a box with his hands.

I got a couple of minutes to tell my sad tale; then Professor Piper, who had finally begun to focus his attention on the brighter possibilities of the following morning, took over a small but very attentive class, which didn't recess until almost dark. Since this is only one of many turkey tales, I'll just sum up some of this old Prof's sage advice for new turkey hunters with a few comments of my own:

Piper: "Appreciating the almost unbelievable sharpness of the eye of the gobbler may be the most important factor in turkey hunting. Scientific studies show that an old gobbler can spot an object, focus on it, and identify it *ten times* faster than a man can! This means that a gobbler can see more in one second than you can see in ten. So, measures to counter the sharp eye of the gobbler are all important: measures such as good camouflage, a good hiding spot to call from, and, most important of all, being absolutely still as the bird approaches."

My comment: Concur 100%. But never hide *too* good. If you hide so good you can't get your gun up and shoot the bird when he gets in range, as I've done several times, why hide at all? When possible, call from just over a rise or ridge from the bird, so there's no way for him to see you until he pops over the top in easy range. Or, hide behind a log or bush, or put your back against a tree facing the direction you think the gobbler will approach from, and don't move a muscle when he gets close. Even with the gobbler's big edge in eyesight, if he's moving and you're still, you'll usually see him first.

Piper: "Most spring gobblers are far easier to call up than most hunters realize. Most hunters can learn to use one of the various type callers effectively in a few days—*if* they *work* and if they have live turkeys or a good recording of turkey calls to work with."

My comment: Concur—with those qualifications spelled out in Chapter 2.

Piper: "Learning only the simple love yelp of the hen can get most new hunters a spring gobbler. But a purr or muffled yelp will often help pull him in, too."

My comment: Concur. But in my opinion, purrs are rarely necessary. And never yelp *until* the bird leaves his roost. While he's still in the tree, he knows any real hen around will only cluck—so this is what the hunter should also do. Then yelp only when you *know* he's on the ground.

Piper: "A mouth diaphragm caller is the most effective calling instrument because its tone is highly realistic. And because it's held in the mouth, the hands are always free to hold the gun."

My comment: Concur—*if* you have a good musical ear and can learn to use a mouth caller. But once again let me stress that many hunters, including myself, just can't learn to use that type caller. And we kill our share of turkeys with boxes, suction callers, slates, and tubes.

Piper: (Plug) "I honestly believe that our Penn's Woods mouth yelpers and slate callers, our True Tone boxes, our EZY Tube caller, and our Tom Terpin wing-bone type yelpers are the best calls on the market today—and our new 'Expert Turkey Calling' record is also the best. Be sure and tell your readers that Penns Woods Products (Delmont, Pa.) can really help them with their turkey calling."

My comment: The new Penn's Woods record is superb. And all their callers are good. But I also like the World Champion box made by M. L. Lynch. And my favorite yelper is that plastic tube caller made by Harold Knight of Cadiz, Kentucky.

Just before dark Frank and I hit the woods hoping to hear an old gobbler give his position away by gobbling when he flew up to roost. Regardless of what you hear to the contrary, even Eastern gobblers often roost in the same spot night after night. Many such toms I have bagged over the years have done so. Unfortunately for the hunter, they don't always announce their presence in roost areas in the evening. But one of Frank's old toms was as cooperative that evening as he had been in the moonlight the night before. He gobbled twice in the exact spot where he had roosted the past two nights—and Frank's morale shot to dizzy new heights. I failed to hear a bird, and went to bed biting my fingernails.

I had a good sleep anyway, mainly because I began thinking about those swelling numbers of old radar-eyed toms
saturating many turkey woods from coast to coast, and how
they'll be providing hunting's greatest thrill to eager young
hunters following us. It was good to also know that concerned
pros like Frank Piper were at last proving to young hunters
everywhere that turkey calling is no difficult and mysterious art,
but a simple skill which any serious hunter can master. I finally
dozed off picturing the millions of thundering gobbles I hoped
new hunters would thrill to in the years to come—and praying
I would hear *just one* the next morning.

A full hour before daylight, Frank and Lamar marched
briskly into the darkness for their final rendezvous with destiny.
I tried to get Hans to follow me around with his camera in case
I should luck out on a gobbler, too. But he announced, "There's
no way! I'm gonna call my *own* gobbler up and shoot him
with my camera. *Then,* if I hear you working a bird, I'll ease
up and record your performance on film." I gave up. Hearing
those gobbles the morning before had driven our cameraman
completely nutty.

On my mountaintop, daylight crept in this time with fore-
boding stillness. Neither the close-in old tom nor the young
bird below said a word—and I heard not the faintest gobble in
the direction Frank and Lamar were working.

Then I *thought* I heard a faint gobble far below the mountain to the southeast. I looked at those almost straight down
ridges and thought of the hell it would be to get back up them.
But I was a desperate man, so down I went.

For an hour I plunged downward, sweating and listening
at strategic points. Once I heard three distant shots echo from
the general direction I was headed, and I almost turned back.
Finally, I reached a long ridge overlooking a small creek, and
I heard beautiful music. Two gobblers were sounding off
a quarter mile ahead and near the bottom of the creek. I
hit the creek bottom, where there was a fair amount of
cover, and moved in. By the time I closed to reasonable
calling range, the birds had moved up a steep open ridge
on my left. Their continuous gobbles told me they had set
up a strutting area near the ridgetop. I knew they would

be hard to budge from that spot, especially if I tried to call them downhill; but in that area the ridge was far too open and dry to climb without spooking the birds. So, I chanced a few calls to try to lure the toms to the bottom. This failing, I turned and back-tracked up the creek.

Finally, I reached a gully running up the ridge the gobblers were on, and about a half-mile away from their position. Knowing the gobblers couldn't spot or hear me climbing the gully, I headed uphill. Reaching the rocky ridgetop, which also was fairly open and covered with dry leaves, I eased toward the rattling on all fours. Because of the dry, open, and noisy terrain, I stopped about 400 yards short of the birds. Another shallow gully cut the ridgetop about halfway between my position and that of the birds, but I hoped I could call them across that. I lay on my stomach on a slight rise behind a log. From this calling position, the birds couldn't spot me until they climbed into shooting range.

I started to make my first call—then began to worry. Could these be the same two birds Frank and Lamar were working? I was unsure of my position after the long winding descent down the mountain. I *thought* I was well north and east of the cabin and the gobblers that Frank and Lamar were going to work. But I had moved a long way in the last hour, and those gobblers could have moved a long way, too. So, I listened intently to make sure that no one else was trying to call the birds. Hearing no one else, I went to work. The range was long for my tube, but the woods were open and I judged correctly that the gobblers could hear it.

The first series of loud yelps from the tube stimulated immediate and passionate replies from both birds. But I was supposed to come to them. They continued to gobble almost incessantly, and I refused to answer for ten minutes. Then, I let go with three more yelps to let them know I wasn't budging either. This sequence of events recurred another three or four times, until finally the gobblers could stand the pressure no longer.

There was a long pause, then a muffled gobble, and I knew at least one of the birds was in the shallow gully enroute to me.

On my elbows, I eased my old twelve across the log—and waited. A long two minutes later, the white-topped head and wide tail fan of a strutting gobbler popped into view above the rocky slope below. I eased the barrel a few inches to the right and squeezed off the charge of #6's. As I struggled to my feet, I heard a winged explosion at the point of aim and watched a black blur sailing downhill well out of range.

There was no sound of a head-shot gobbler threshing in the dry leaves. How could I have missed the bird at 30 yards? Then I walked down to the spot where the bird was standing

Frank Piper brings his big gobbler to my camper where mine is already hanging. I had to climb a mountain to get above my gobbler before I could tube him in. Frank had to cross a creek to get his, after failing to entice him across the creek the previous morning.

when I fired—and there he lay, still and magnificent! Then I knew it was the other gobbler that had flushed when I shot.

I had been too busy racing down those winding ridges to check my compass, and had no clear idea of where the cabin lay. So, I tied my trophy's head and a foot together with a piece of my undershirt, making it easier to carry as a sling, and headed for the Jeep. They say that a 20-pound gobbler with a ten-inch beard is never heavy if he's carried by the hunter who bagged him. This is not quite true. But after three hours of easing uphill a few yards at a time, and stopping for long rests and the privilege of stroking those beautiful iridescent feathers, I finally made the Jeep in sky-high spirits and little worse for wear.

My tom had the longest spurs, but Frank's had the best beard.

When I reached the cabin, all was quiet, but hanging in the front yard was another monster gobbler, one which put even my trophy to shame. Its jet black beard was almost as thick as a man's wrist—and *twelve* inches long! At that moment, Frank and Hans materialized in the edge of the cabin clearing wearing ear-to-ear grins.

One look at the sparkle in Frank's eyes told me that he had bagged the monster, and that he was on Cloud 9, too. The three shots I had heard enroute to my gobbler had been his. With Lamar 20 yards ahead of him, Frank was calling from the opposite ridge just above the roosting spot of the two near-camp gobblers. And the old bird had slunk by Lamar without being detected. Frank spotted him in full strut about midway between his position and that of his partner's. At that moment, Lamar turned his head slightly and the gobbler sold out—and Frank jumped up, stumbling and shooting, and managed to down him.

Lamar, who had pressing business at the office, had already managed to tear himself loose from his new-found turkey heaven, and was jetting back to New York. But Frank said he left with his pocket bulging with slates and boxes and a diaphragm in his mouth—which is good news for all turkey nuts like me who think there should be at least three or four turkey stories in every issue of every outdoor magazine.

CHAPTER 9

How Three Alabama
Gobblers Lost Their Beards

Max parked the pick-up on top of the high hill, and we eased down the old logging road toward the swamp. Our timing was perfect. The March sky was just beginning to turn gray. And it was one of those perfect gobbling mornings—clear, crisp, and still.

Before we were halfway down the hill, a thundering gobble shattered the stillness. "Gosh-a-mighty!" Max whispered. "He's ready for action early this morning!" Again the gobbler sounded off. He was roosting on a ridge about a quarter mile ahead and just to our right. I knew what Max was going to whisper next and it suited me fine. "If it's O.K. with you, I'll take the swamp clearing and you can have the ridge."

I nodded, cut into the woods, and headed for a calling position close to the gobbler and on his contour. Guided by the tom's frequent and fervent rattles, I fought my way up the steep ridge side through tangles of briars and scrub oak. A few minutes later, I was behind a big stump overlooking a fairly open slope about 200 yards from the gobbler's position. By this time, I knew Max was on station at the fringe of the little swamp clearing some 300 yards below. Our duel was about to begin.

I decided to play my trump card before Max went to work. Just before the sun popped over the big oaks beyond the swamp, I cupped my box tightly and stroked out two faint and sleepy clucks. The tom answered with a booming double-gobble and I could almost see him prancing back and forth on the roost limb in a cocky half-strut.

I waited for five minutes as the top of the sun eased into view shooting streaks of fire across the sky. Birdsong crescendoed and squirrels began to chatter. Just as I started to call again, I heard Max yelp from below, and at the same moment I heard a faint whirr and knew the gobbler had left the roost. I strained my eyes to pick up the big bird in his silent glide, but he appeared neither in my area nor over the trees he would have to top if he were winging his way to the swamp below. A few seconds later, a muffled gobble rang out, and I knew the tom had glided down in the immediate vicinity of his roost tree.

My odds for calling a gobbler in could not have been higher. He was on the ground not 200 yards away, on the same contour I was on, and he had to believe there was a young hen nearby. To confirm his belief into positive knowledge, I tried three more seductive yelps—this time with the tube. Then I laid down the call and picked up my twelve. Again the tom answered with a shattering double-gobble. A few minutes later he appeared in the clearing edge and pranced slowly toward me in full strut. I was frozen with only the tip of my gun barrel and my eyes and camouflaged cap protruding above the stump. Closer and closer the big bird came until he was just out of gun range. His chestnut tail was spread in a magnificent fan, and I could hear his booming strut.

Then, Max let go with another series of perfect pleading "Kee-oaks" with his mouth diaphragm. The old tom dropped his strut and stretched his long neck in Max's direction. A second later, my trophy turned and headed downhill. I had just witnessed a most vivid and painful demonstration of the effectiveness of a diaphragm in the mouth of a real expert.

For a long five minutes, complete and suspense-loaded stillness prevailed. Then three self-explanatory sounds occurred in rapid succession. First, Max's "Kee-oak, kee-oak, kee-oak"—then a thundering gobble—then the boom of Max's twelve gauge. I waited another hour, but heard nothing except the sound of Max driving the pick-up down the hill to the swamp clearing below.

Shortly thereafter, I accepted defeat and headed downhill through the emerald pines and oaks now bathed in brilliant sunlight.

When I reached the pick-up, Max was leaning against the tailgate, drinking coffee. The grin on his broad leathery face confirmed his success. I pretended to be half-mad. "Well, congratulations, Old Buddy! I guess you know you stole that old tom right out of my lap!"

"Well, you know what they always say—'May the best man win!' But what do you mean—"old" tom? That shows what you know about turkeys. He's a tom all right—but not exactly a granddaddy!"

I looked in the back of the pick-up and saw that the tom was a young bird with a three or four inch beard. "But I gotta admit," Max continued, "he was the loudest gobbling young tom I ever heard. When he sounded off that last time, he had slipped up behind me and wasn't 10 feet away. I was so shook up, I nearly missed him."

On the way back to camp, Max and I were silent for a long time. We were both thinking about a stalwart young six-footer who had elected to hunt alone that morning.

Finally, I said what we were both thinking.

"I sure hope Richard scored. Any kid who flies all the way back from an overseas station to the wilds of Alabama, instead of taking his R and R in glamorous Tokyo or Honolulu sure deserves to get his first gobbler."

"That he does," Max agreed, and his blue eyes lit up. "If hard hunting will get Richard a tom, he'll make the grade. Even if he is my boy, I've got to admit that I've never seen a more independent or harder hunter. Except for lousy luck and the fact that he won't take help from anyone, he'd have killed his tom long before he went overseas."

It was noon before Richard made it back to the hunting cabin. He was empty-handed but we could see by the excited glint in his eyes that he, too, had been in gobbler country. Max couldn't stand it any longer. "Well, tell us about it!"

Richard pumped himself a quart of cold spring water, lowered his lofty frame into a porch chair, and entertained us with a tale of three big gobblers rattling off all at once around his daylight calling position.

"It was cool—just like I dreamed about all those long nights overseas. I had three big gobblers coming to me at the same time. Two of them were coming straight for me in full strut —but they were joined by a couple of hens just before they got in gun range. They stayed just out of range in full strut and gobbled their heads off for at least thirty minutes. All this time, I could hear the third gobbler moving in from behind me. When I finally guessed he was close enough to shoot, I eased around just in time to see him explode from a clump of brush and sell out for tall timber. The other gobblers heard his ruckus and they flushed, too. I spent the rest of the morning trying to call one of 'em back, but naturally I didn't make the grade."

"Why don't you let Dave or me go with you in the morning, and do the calling," Max suggested. "After all, you only have two days left."

"No, sir!" Richard retorted. "I'm going to call up my own gobbler—or *never* get one!"

Richard and I did some independent scouting that afternoon, and I was lucky enough to hear several birds fly up in the edge of a big swamp about a half-mile from where Max had nailed his gobbler that morning. Richard saw two big gobblers just before dark, so he also had his hunting area for the next morning pinpointed. After a big dinner, we turned in early for a good night's sleep.

I've enjoyed spring gobbler hunting with Max Davis, a timber dealer who lives in Andalusia, Alabama, for many years, and with our mutual friend Don Thomas. Both are real experts with the mouth diaphragm and know every inch of that vast stretch of turkey-loaded woods in the Andalusia area.

Max, Don, and I often hunt the Blue Springs Management Area, just south of Andalusia, which is one of the best public turkey hunting areas anywhere in the country. But during this spring hunt, Max, Richard and I were hunting on nearby

This young Alabama tom came within six feet of my calling spot when I was hunting with camera only. Again, it was those sweet tube yelps that brought him in.

private lands leased by the Little Pine Hunting Club, of which Max is a member and also Chief Game Warden.

Richard had been away at school for several years, then overseas with his military unit, but on this our first hunt together, we hit it off from the start, as avid turkey hunters, young and old, are bound to do. I went to sleep that night dreaming of big black gobblers—strutting, gobbling, and coming to my call—but hoping even more, that one would come to Richard's box.

A little creek, not ten feet wide, cost me my gobbler the second morning. As I approached the creek near the point where it entered the swamp, the old tom sounded off from a finger ridge slanting into the swamp just beyond the creek. Rather than taking a chance on spooking the roosting bird, I tried to do the almost impossible: I tried to call him across the creek. And, of course, I failed. After leaving the roost, he hung up just across the creek, gobbled his head off for fifteen minutes, then departed, still gobbling occasionally, along a main ridge paralleling the swamp. I was unable to get ahead of him.

Richard also failed to make the grade that second morning, and a heavy rain prevented us from scouting in the afternoon. That night we engaged in skull practice which we hoped would help Richard collect his beard the next and final morning.

We got up at the usual 4 a.m. After a quick hot breakfast, Richard once more headed out on foot in the star-studded darkness. I drove my 4-wheel drive to the edge of the big swamp, close to the spot where I had heard the tom the morning before.

It was another perfect gobbling morning. Not a breath of wind touched the big woods still bathed in yellow moonlight. I worked slowly along the swamp edge and damp leaves kept my movement completely silent. I thought about the big rattler I had killed in this same area the season before, but being a turkey hunter, I focused my attention on more important matters—and plowed ahead.

Light began to filter into the swamp and off to my right a horned owl began to hoot its eerie mating call. I stopped for a moment and listened intently, but no gobble challenged the owl's hoots. I continued on and finally reached the little stream that had cost me my gobbler the morning before. If he was roosting on the same ridge just across the creek, I would be in a more favorable calling position this time. I waded the creek, climbed above his probable roosting area, and waited in the center of a fallen pine top.

Dawn slipped in with rapidly changing hues of red, orange, and silver. Mysterious shadows and silhouettes slowly turned into a panorama of gnarled hardwoods, green pines, and dogwoods with snow-white crowns. The familiar forest symphony began, first with the tinkling chirp of a swamp wren. Then song birds of all sorts began to warble their welcome to spring, and squirrels began to chatter, and bobwhites added their flute-like notes, and raucous crows, hammering woodpeckers, and loud-mouthed owls took over the thundering lead. Then suddenly, "GIL-OBBLE-OBBLE-OBBLE! GIL-OBBLE-OBBLE-OBBLE!" The king musician rocked the woods with his fearful call.

Except for the pounding of my heart, the forest was now completely quiet. Then again the old king rattled off, "GIL-OBBLE-OBBLE-OBBLE! GIL-OBBLE-OBBLE-OBBLE!" He was on the same roosting throne he had occupied the morning before—about 200 yards straight down the finger ridge from my new position.

The sun was completely up, but I could tell by the way he gobbled that the old tom was still prancing up and down on the limb of his roost tree. I cupped my box tightly and gave him a couple of low clucks. Then beyond the thin shield of brush I was peering through, I saw him fly straight up the ridge toward me. He hit the ground in a patch of sunlight 100 yards below and put up his long warty periscope. After stretching his great wings, he let go with another thundering gobble and went into full strut.

For the next ten minutes, the old tom and I played a game of stalemate. Each time I yelped, he would peer in my direction, then gobble back. But he wouldn't come a step closer than that secure patch of sunlight he was strutting in 100 yards below. I had run into an educated and call-shy old bird that wasn't about to come to the tube music he had heard the morning before. So, I pocketed the tube and used my slate.

The old tom started toward me. The slate had convinced him I was a new and very real hen. He pranced slowly into a small clearing almost in range. My hands were now on the gun and I was ready.

At that moment, I heard a noise to my left. Out of the corner of my eye I saw a young gobbler coming out of the swamp headed straight for me! I knew the old gobbler would spook if the young tom saw me and flushed. I remained frozen, concentrating on the old gobbler, but watching the young tom, too. I hoped the young tom would pass on by, but no such luck. He was eager for a hen, too, and his only objective was to get to me before the old gobbler did. I did a crash staff study. If this hadn't been my last day to hunt, I would have taken the old gobbler or nothing. But since time was running out, I decided to take the young tom if he spooked the old gobbler.

The young tom threw on the brakes not ten feet from me and peered into the treetop. Suddenly, he made me out, and let go with a loud "PUTT!" Then, at the same instant, both gobblers flushed. The old gobbler was still out of sure range and the young gobbler was boring straight up over my head too close to shoot. I waited for a long second for the young tom to get a bit further away—which was almost an irretrievable mistake. He put a big pine trunk between us and I had to jump sideways and shoot at the same time. Somehow, I managed to down him.

I raced down the ridge with my gun ready, but the gobbler was still. He lay on a patch of white sand at the base of a big cypress—a streamlined mass of iridescent beauty with a four inch beard. He was one of the largest and most beautifully plumaged young gobblers I had ever taken. As I looked at the handsome bird, I had only one regret: that this great experience could not have been Richard's. I knew that spring turkey hunting was just too tough for all three of us to fill out on one spring hunt.

Max was having breakfast when I got back to the cabin. We patted each other on the back and gloated over our mutual successes like old turkey hunting cronies are prone to do. And

This is the young Alabama tom I finally settled for after being outfoxed by an old monster. Both Max and Richard Davis got their gobblers, too, on the same hunt.

we took pictures and spun old tales about other hunts and other gobblers we had fooled and been fooled by.

Finally, we saw movement down an old logging road leading toward the area where Richard was hunting. A set of green Army fatigues slowly materialized and we walked down the road toward them. Then we made out a big ball of black under Richard's arm. The impossible had happened. Our hero had scored, too!

If there were three happier hunters in those big Alabama woods that day, I don't know where you would have found them. Max and I hung onto every word as Richard told us how he was calling up his first gobbler, another fine young tom, when suddenly it quit gobbling . . . "After twenty minutes, I had given up and decided to change calling positions. When I stood up, I heard a noise behind me and caught a glimpse of the tom, which had circled, racing through the brush. I had only one chance at him as he shot through a small clearing—but somehow I managed to see his beard and bowl him over! What a day!"

When I left Andalusia, Richard was trying to decide if he could work out a way to take his gobbler back overseas with him. If Richard's buddies didn't get roast turkey, I'm sure they did get a hair-raising account of a great Alabama gobbler hunt.

If you would like to hunt this same great southern Alabama turkey country, write the Manager, Blue Springs Wildlife Management Area, or the Andalusia Chamber of Commerce, Andalusia, Alabama, 36420. They will give you the information you need for a great hunt.

CHAPTER 10

Spring Hunting Tips Straight From The Gobbler's Mouth

The last twinkling stars flickered out as I huffed and puffed my way to the ridgetop. I sat down in the soft cradle of a decaying stump and waited for the sky to silver. Fifty yards down the ridge was the saddle that Sonny Glenn had told me the old Mississippi tom would be roosting near.

The sky brightened and the early morning symphony of birdsong began. Silhouettes of pines began to take on color and my heart beat faster and faster. I could now see that the ridge ended just beyond the saddle—and I knew it would be difficult to hear the gobbler if he were roosting low in that direction. The perfect listening point would be on the *other* side of the saddle near the point where the ridge dropped off.

Twice I started to head for this better listening point— but each time I remembered Sonny's warning that the old gobbler might be roosting right at the saddle. The sun was now almost up and still I hadn't heard a gobble. At this point, I couldn't resist easing down the ridge toward the better listening point.

Just as I reached the center of the saddle, I heard a sharp "PUTT!", then the whirr of exploding wings almost so close I could touch them. The old tom had leaped out of a nearby pine almost at eyeball level. By the time I got over the shock, threw off the safety, and made positive identification, the range was questionable and I let my trophy go. Had I stayed hidden and still in my original calling spot, the old tom would probably have flown straight to me.

This old tom re-emphasized a turkey hunting lesson I should have learned years before. Let's call it LESSON #1: *Don't Try To Get Too Close To A Gobbler.* Trying to get too

Don't try to get too close to a gobbling tom, especially during the bright hours.

close to a gobbler is a mistake made all too often—either when you know where a tom's roosting or when you just hear him sound off. I remember spooking a Virginia tom off his roost a good half hour before the first crack of dawn. I had heard him gobble at dusk the evening before and tried to get too close, believing my movements wouldn't alarm him while it was still dark. But the old tom heard me climbing through the dry leaves and I heard him flush in the dark some 200 yards away.

In the future, if I err, it will be in the side of my calling position being too *far* away—not too close! If you spook a wiley tom by trying to get too close, you have *no* chance to bag him. If you're a bit too far away, you have some chance. If the country is thick and brushy, or if there's a ridge between us, or if it's still early and visibility is poor, I'll try for about 200 yards. But, if the terrain is flat and fairly open and visibility is good, I'll settle for about 400. This is one lesson I think I've *finally* learned from old gobblers. The great turkey country I learned this lesson in was the Tombigbee River bottom near Columbus.

LESSON #2: *Sometimes It Takes An Odd Ball Call To Lure In A Trophy Tom.* As already stressed, the love yelp of the hen, used alone or in conjunction with an occasional cluck, will bring in far more spring gobblers than any other call. However, there is no single calling rule that applies to all gobblers. For some unknown reason, an occasional old tom will refuse to answer or come to traditional mating calls—and yet gobble his head off at some other call spring turkey hunters seldom use—then come straight to it.

Two old toms recently taught me this lesson well. The first was the king of Alabama's Tuskegee National Forest. I heard this old bird sound off from his roost for two mornings in a row, but was unable to make him respond to my best rendered yelps. Late the second afternoon, I decided to try to roost the old tom and moved into the swamp where he had been gobbling both preceding mornings.

About a half hour before sundown, I found a good hiding place on a little knoll just above a line of thick underbrush in the swamp bottom. Afternoon hunting in Alabama was legal and I pulled out my tube and yelped a couple of times hoping I might get lucky enough to get an answer. This failing, I clucked on my box loudly twice in rapid succession. Immediately a turkey answered with two identical "Clucks" about 200 yards on the other side of the brush.

A few minutes later, I clucked again and *again* got immediate response—this time less than 100 yards away. I clucked one more time and picked up my gun. The air was filled with the staccato of cracking underbrush and continual sharp clucks drawing closer and closer. I pointed my gun in the direction of the noise and a few seconds later, I was looking down my barrel at a magnificent gobbler. He was coming so fast that I believe he would have run over me if I hadn't stopped him with a charge of #6's.

This had to be the same old monarch I had heard gobbling the two mornings before which wouldn't pay one iota of attention to my conventional hen yelps. Would he have come to *clucks* during our two early morning duels? I'll never know for sure—but my guess is he might have.

An even more radical spring call by my good friend Joe Meeks, ramrod of Tellico Junction Hunting Preserve in Englewood, Tennessee, got me another recent gobbler. I was visiting Joe to help him work out a program for tutoring gun and bowhunters in the art of turkey calling. After we had finished our business, Joe told me that a big spooky tom had been loose on the large preserve for six months and no one had been able to bag him. It didn't take me long to agree to help Joe solve this tough problem. Joe had heard the old gobbler on his roost a couple of mornings before and that's exactly where we were at first light the next day.

We didn't hear the gobbler there, and proceeded to climb one ridge after another to listen. By 9 a.m., the evasive tactics of that old pen-raised bird were clearly established. Just as we were about to give up, we heard the old tom sound off about 300 yards below us in a thick stream bed. I grinned at Joe. "He's really ready! It should take me about five minutes to have him in our laps." Boy, was I cocky!

I extracted my old faithful tube and let go with as sexy a run of hen yelps as I've ever sent through the spring woods. I waited. But nothing happened. Again, I let go with love music that no gobbler on the ground should be able to resist. And, again the old tom said not a word in reply. After three or four more unsuccessful attempts, I put my call in my pocket and shook my head.

At that point Joe pulled out a battered old Tom Gaskins box and said, "Let me give him a try." Joe didn't yelp with his box—and he didn't even cluck with it. Instead, he let go with a series of squeaky, ear-splitting *cackles!* Until this moment, I would have sworn that no turkey hunter in his right mind would ever use such a call in the spring and that no self-respecting gobbler would answer it—but I was dead wrong. The old gobbler answered that off-beat call with one of the loudest double-gobbles I've ever heard.

I couldn't believe what was happening. I tried a run of my old faithful yelps twice more. But the old gobbler would pay absolutely no attention whatsoever to them. It really hurt when Joe finally called in the old gobbler with those ungodly cackles—and I had to shoot a bird which I couldn't call in myself.

I'll still stick with my conventional yelps *most* of the time when hunting spring gobblers. But as these two experiences suggest, when a gobbler hangs up hard in the future, I won't hesitate long before I try more clucking and even cackling. I suggest that you other old gobbler chasers do the same.

LESSON #3: *Choose A Good Calling Position And Stick With It!* I remember well two old toms that taught me this vital lesson. One was a resident of North Carolina's rugged and mountainous Standing Indian Wildlife Management Area west of Franklin. Even before I had a chance to duel with him, this old gobbler nearly got me *drowned.* On the first evening at Standing Indian, I heard this old tom gobble three times when he went to roost. I carefully marked his position about half way up a 1000 foot ridge across the rushing Nantahala River from the trail where I was listening. I checked the river before dark and picked out a point where I could easily ford it. It rained all that night—but, of course, the next morning I tried to cross the river before daylight anyway.

I knew the river was up some, but I didn't realize that it

had risen three feet during the dark night. When I felt the rushing water almost at my wader tops, I started to turn back. But knowing the old tom was waiting for me on the mountain-side just across the swirling waters was too much. I tried to inch on across. Then, I hung one of my boots in a crevice and was swept under. I managed to fight the current and to get back to shore about 50 yards downstream—wringing wet and so cold I had to give up the hunt that morning.

A couple of days later, the stream level had lowered so I could cross it. The old gobbler was roosting in the same area. He opened up with two loud gobbles just as it was beginning to get light. He was about ¼ mile straight above me under a rocky knob. I worked my way quickly up a ridge leading well to the right of his position. I found a perfect hiding place in a fallen treetop almost on the same contour the old tom was on and about 300 yards from him. He was gobbling from the roost the entire fifteen minutes it took me to get to my calling position.

I eased out my box and clucked softly. He answered with a booming gobble. Then a few minutes later, he gobbled again. This time his thunder was muffled and I knew he had flown down from his roost. Then I gave him a run of hen yelps with my tube. And again, he answered with uncontrollable passion.

The old bird moved back and forth along a 100 yard strutting area and hung up there. For nearly an hour, he would answer my every yelp—but wouldn't come any closer. It was then that I made the foolhardy mistake of trying to ease down the brushy ridge to a new calling point closer to him. I had just left my position when the gobbler sounded off again—this time not more than 100 yards away. I was caught flat-footed —he was coming straight for me and all I could do was to lie down in the open. To make matters worse, a doe about 50 yards to my right had caught my movement and was beginning to snort like a banshee. For five minutes the doe continued to snort and to point me like a bird dog. Naturally, the old gobbler got her message and I heard him no more.

If I had stuck with my original excellent and well concealed calling position, it is almost certain that the old tom would have come to me and that the doe would not have seen me. I should have been smart enough to learn then and there the lesson that old North Carolina gobbler tried to teach me. Yet, it took a second lesson a few weeks later from a Virginia tom in the east edge of George Washington National Forest to drive home the point that a gobbler chaser should stick with a good calling position and not uproot himself from it prematurely.

Fred Kesting, Associate Editor of *Sports Afield*, was accompanying me to listen to gobbler music and to see how a hunter calls in an old tom. After some two hours of maneuvering up and down steep ridges, wading creeks, and bulldozing through brush, we finally got within calling range of an old gobbler singing out with beautiful gusto. "Come and get me if you can!"

The old tom was about 200 yards beyond us and on the same ridgetop we were on. He answered my every yelp, but like the old Standing Indian gobbler, he set up a strutting pattern where he was—and refused to budge from it. One end of the pattern, which lay perpendicular to a line from our position, carried him down into the bed of a creek and the other to the top of the ridge ahead.

After nearly an hour of listening to the old tom move in the same groove, back and forth from the ridgetop to the creek bottom, I decided to leave Fred at our well shielded calling position and to ease on up the ridge the next time I heard the gobbler sound off from the brushy creek bottom. Then I would bushwack him when he came back up the ridge. This tactic appeared to work perfectly. I was now well hidden and within gun range of the upper end of the old tom's strutting pattern.

I gave the old gobbler one series of yelps and picked up my gun. There was a long silence and I knew I would spot the old gobbler's head bobbing up the ridge any second. But the next sound I heard was a booming strut directly behind me. I eased my head around and saw the old tom with every beautiful feather erect—within range and looking back at the bush I had just departed from. But I couldn't shoot for fear of hitting Fred. The old gobbler moved out of sight, then again came into view prancing directly toward Fred. He knew exactly where I had been calling from and was looking for that hen.

A few minutes later, I heard a sharp "PUTT!" and knew the old gobbler had identified my companion. I waited for fifteen minutes, then hoping the gobbler had not spooked out of the country, I yelped again. This time the gobbler answered from about 200 yards down the opposite side of the ridge. He double-gobbled to another yelp—then again reappeared within range, but directly between Fred and me. This time the old gobbler was staring straight at me—and he figured me out. He threw down his head and shot down the ridge like a grey-hound. I jumped to my feet, got one glimpse of his blur—and fired—but missed.

When an old gobbler hangs up and you're in a good calling position, *wait him out.* Had I done this, I probably would have had the beards of both these old natives of North Carolina and Virginia hanging on my wall. When an old gobbler sets up a strutting pattern and refuses to budge from it, he does so because he knows a well mannered hen should come to him. Even the male turkey has his pride. But, if the fair lady refuses to come, the old gobbler will eventually give up and go to her. You may have to out-wait the old sultan for an hour or even two. But do just that, as I intend to in the future. It's our best chance of collecting a beard.

LESSON #4: *Don't Shoot Through Brush With Gun Or Bow.* Two ancient and long bearded southern Alabama gobblers, residing in Blue Springs Management Area near Andalusia, gave me a thorough lesson on this subject. I was calling from a clump of oaks on the edge of a small clearing. I had been talking with both these old birds for about thirty minutes and they had answered me in unison every time I yelped, coming closer and closer. When they stepped into the far corner of the small green clearing, with white heads bobbing and long beards almost dragging the ground, my heart pounded like a bass drum and my hands began shaking as though I had never seen a gobbler before.

Suddenly, four hens also stepped out on the sunlit stage—and both gobblers went into full strut. Greens, golds, and purples sparkled from the broad blackness of their breasts and their chestnut tails were handsome, quivering fans that should have made every hen in the clearing swoon. But the hens were coy and aloof. They paid no attention to the passionate gobblers and began pecking daintily at grass seeds and clover.

I now knew why the gobblers had been answering my calls—it was early in the season and the hens with them were not yet ready for lovemaking. I was in a fairly good calling position—*if* the gobblers came in right. From their position on the side of the clearing to my right, I was fairly well shielded by brush but I knew the old sharp-eyed toms would detect any appreciable move I might make. I had a clear view of the side of the clearing to my left and decided to chance one more series of yelps before the birds could move in that part of the clearing and have an open view of me.

I waited until the prancing gobblers turned away from me and dropped their heads behind their towering tails. And I made sure that the heads of all the hens were down feeding. At that moment, I eased my tube to my lips and floated two soft yelps to the old toms. Immediately they both roared back with excited gobbles and turned in my direction.

For the next thirty minutes the old toms were torn between moving over to the brush to check me out—and trying to arouse the passions of the four hens on the other side of them. They would strut in my direction until they were 50 or 60 yards away, then turn and move back toward the hens, both sounding off with thundering gobbles every few minutes. Now that I had focused the attention of the gobblers on my exact position, I hardly dared move a muscle. But one time, when they were moving away from me and I was sure the hens were preoccupied with food, I eased my call down and got both hands on my gun. Then I froze and waited the old toms out.

Two or three times the gobblers approached to within 40 yards of my position, but always in that part of the clearing shielded by brush. On the last approach I spotted the hens walk out of the far side of the clearing in the same direction they had come from. One of the hens yelped and both gobblers momentarily broke strut and turned in her direction.

Figuring this might well be my last opportunity, I eased the gun up, put the bead on the neck of the gobbler nearest me, and squeezed off through the brush. All heck broke loose as I tried to get out of the thick oaks and get off a second shot. In the confusion I got a glimpse of one tom running into the brush to my right and the other flushing into the woods on the opposite side of the clearing.

I couldn't believe that my charge of #6's hadn't killed that gobbler at 40 steps. But it hadn't! That wall of brush I was shooting through had deflected those pellets which should have ended up in the old tom's head and neck. It would have done the same to an arrow. In fact, I've lost three toms I called in to easy range because my arrow also was deflected by a twig or limb.

LESSON #5: *Don't Give Up When Your Tom Won't Gobble.* When you have an old tom's general range located, either through finding his sign or through hearing him gobble, you have a good chance to call him in and bag him even if he won't gobble the day you're hunting. In past years, many old toms taught me this lesson—and I took more than a few of them that never said a word. But one of the biggest old South Florida swamp gobblers I've ever dueled really impressed this lesson on me.

Turkey pro "extra-ordinary" Tom Gaskins of Palmdale, Florida and inventor of the famous Gaskins box caller, showed me where this old gobbler was ranging in a long swamp fringed by palmettos. The first morning I listened for this jet-black swamp tom, he sounded off right on schedule. It was barely dawn and he began gobbling with all the enthusiasm you would expect of any red-blooded gobbler on a crisp and still spring morning.

The first time I clucked, he gobbled back as though it sounded so good he couldn't stand it. And the second time, I heard him fly to the ground in my direction. I then yelped, and picked up my gun. He gobbled twice more coming straight for the open area in front of my thick palmetto blind. That was the last time I heard that foxy old bird gobble. But

Toms will sometimes strut all morning and never gobble. If you know you're in a gobbler's area, stay in one place, call occasionally, and wait your quarry out. When the old bird's hens leave, he'll probably come straight to you.

a few seconds later I heard him busting through the palmettos not ten feet behind my back. Knowing the old bird was that close, I figured there was no way he could get away. I stood up and eased the gun in the direction of the noise. Although I heard him racing through the waist-high palmetto clumps at point-blank range, I never saw even one of his black feathers.

I spent four more mornings listening and calling in that area but never heard the old tom utter another sound, either on the roost or in response to my calls. Yet, each morning when I gave up and looked around, I could find fresh tracks where the old tom had approached me—twice so close I could have bagged him if I could have spotted him.

That night, I made the mistake of deciding to give up on that old uncooperative tom and to look for a new one the next day. About that time, two young hunters drove into camp, one of whom had never called up or killed a turkey. I tutored this young man on calling for an hour or so. Then I told him if he was willing to sit all day on the same stump in the same palmetto clump I had been calling from that he might get a shot at this trophy. I suggested that he call occasionally, hold all movement to a minimum, and not raise his gun unless the tom came into full view—in easy range. I was advising this young man on what *I* should have done.

When I finally dragged myself back into camp empty-handed the next night, there was a note on my camper. It read: "Thanks, Mister. He weighed 21 pounds, had a 12-inch beard, and came without gobbling once." I later confirmed this wise and patient young hunter's claim at the check station. He not only had killed the old tom that I had given up on because he wouldn't gobble, but he had gotten a real trophy: the oldest and largest gobbler killed in Florida's Fisheating Creek Wildlife Management Area that spring.

LESSON #6: *Don't Give Up On A Gobbler Because You Think You've Spooked Him With A Bad Call Or Noise.* Many old gobblers have taught me the truth of this lesson. I've learned that immediately following a bad yelp or cluck with a good one will usually allay the suspicions of an approaching tom—and that he'll sometimes come on in as surely as if he hadn't heard the sour note. Even a noisy Jeep, the slamming of a car door, or the crack of a broken branch under your feet will sometimes fail to spook a wary gobbler.

I was hunting on a private farm in Virginia recently with Tom Rodgers, a real artist with all callers, and President of the National Wild Turkey Federation. Tom was rattling up a steep mountainside with his Jeep in low-low gear. When he reached the top, he decided to call one more time, even though he hadn't heard a gobbler all morning. He shut off the noisy Jeep, then accidentally slammed the door as he got out. Immediately a gobbler roared back at the *slamming door*—and so close it made Tom's hair stand on end.

Although Tom could hardly believe all this was happening and that the gobbler would still respond to a call, he decided to try. Figuring he ought to get at least a few yards away from the Jeep before calling, he eased a short distance down the trail—then stepped into a patch of tall grass for cover. At that moment, his foot punched through a half-decayed log, creating a crack as loud as a shotgun. This time the gobbler gobbled back at the cracking log and almost in gun range. Convinced now that anything was possible with this old gobbler, Tom yelped at him. Almost before he could aim his gun, the old tom was standing there eyeballing him not 30 yards away!

Tom admits that this was not the toughest turkey he's ever killed and says he will be less reluctant to try to work a tom in the future just because he has made a little accidental racket. Me, too! Of course, this had to be an odd-ball old tom that was especially stupid—not sharp and wary as most of his brothers.

LESSON #7: *Don't Shoot Prematurely!* Two old long-bearded tutors drove this all-important lesson home as I dueled them last spring. One was the only gobbler I ever called out of one state and killed in another. I was hunting out of Devil's Dive Resort on Table Rock Lake almost on the Arkansas-Missouri line. The old tom had a habit of roosting near the top of a high ridge in Missouri where the season was still open, but usually flew down and ranged the rest of the day in Arkansas where the season was closed. On two mornings, I succeeded in calling this magnificent bird to within 50 steps in legal Missouri territory, but then he would leave me for a competing hen calling from nearby Arkansas. On both these occasions, I came close to trying the old tom at that considerable range, and my old tight-shooting twelve might have done the job. But I passed up each shot.

On that third morning, the real hen the old tom had been going to in Arkansas had evidently received all the servicing she was interested in. Very early, the gobbler again spurned me for his Arkansas girl friend—but I could tell in a hurry that he hadn't found her. I heard no hen yelps and he was gobbling his head off just over the fence that marked the state line.

I let the old sultan sweat for fifteen or twenty minutes more, then let him have another soft and seductive run of tube yelps. The next time he gobbled he was closer. I yelped once more and picked up my gun. I was well hidden behind a limestone outcropping when his blue-white head bobbled into view. At 40 steps his haughty tiptoeing toward me ceased and he went into full strut. The bright sunlight set every one of his handsome feathers afire, and the hissing sound of his strut was beautiful music.

He pranced closer and closer, until I could almost reach out and touch him. Then he turned and pranced away from me. When he reached 20 steps, I said "PUTT!" His head and neck stretched high, and I fired at his white crown. If I had been impatient, or greedy, as I almost was, and had tried him at those questionable ranges either of the two mornings before, I might have crippled and lost this fine 21-pound trophy with a ten-inch beard.

Another Pennsylvania gobbler ruling the roost a few miles east of Huntington, also taught me the wisdom of always holding out for a sure close-range kill and of never taking a "maybe" shot. I was hunting an area recommended by Paul Hickes of Huntington, one of the finest sportsmen and best turkey hunters I have ever known. During six days of hard hunting, I passed up three gobblers I called to within 50 or 55 yards. By 9 a.m. on the morning of the seventh and last day of my hunt, I had almost given up and was enroute back to camp. I stopped on a high ridge to try one last yelp —and, to my surprise, I was answered by a gobbler far below.

Ten minutes later, I was in good calling position behind a fallen log on an open ridge some 200 yards directly above the point where I estimated the old tom had gobbled from. I yelped with the tube once more, and the gobbler answered. Almost before I could put the tube down and pick up my gun, I saw him coming at a dead run. When the big bird

Unless you have a sure close-range shot, pass it up. The next day may give you a clean kill and eliminate any worry about wounding a majestic gobbler.

stopped and I fired, he was exactly 12 steps away. How glad I was that I had turned down those earlier and questionable shots! I had another real trophy, an 18-pounder with a nine-inch beard—and the satisfaction of knowing that I had bagged him cleanly and really earned him.

LESSON #8: *Beat Competition And "Bad Luck" With Patience And Perseverance.* Roy Orton, who hunted gobblers for the first time during our New York hunt discussed in Chapter 5, worked his heart out for three more springs without scoring. Then he flew down to Florida in hopes that his long period of bad luck would finally change. I had already bagged my two Florida gobblers and I wanted Roy to get his. We opened this hunt on a Saturday in early March in Richloam Wildlife Management Area near Bushnell—and we had plenty of competition. Hunters were camped and hunting everywhere, and for the first three days serious hunting was impossible.

But we stuck it out, spending every minute of daylight each day listening and scouting for sign. And it paid off. Through reading tracks and hearing a couple of gobbles at daylight, we located the roost and range area of two long-bearded professor gobblers in a big dark hardwood hammock. And we learned plenty from them. First, by reading their fresh tracks in the hammock every day, we learned that all those early-season hunters hadn't spooked them out of the country, as most hunters would have believed. The wise old toms merely ducked the hunters, hid until each passed by, then resumed their normal daily movement patterns.

By the fourth day, most of the hunters were gone. That afternoon, with the woods now quiet, we knew we had a good chance to roost one of the old toms. A good two hours before dusk, I took up a listening position on one side of the thick swamp that cut through the center of the big hammock, and Roy headed for the other—without our guns, for only morning hunting was legal.

Just before Roy reached his listening point, he suddenly spotted the fanned tail of one of the big birds strutting in a clearing just ahead. What followed next is a portrait of a real dedicated turkey hunter in action. The woods were so open, Roy knew his only course of action to keep from spooking the gobbler was to hit the ground and freeze. This he did, and with hundreds of mosquitoes drilling him, he lay in that prone position without moving for some two hours while he heard the gobbler strutting all around him. Finally, the woods grew quiet and dark. And Roy heard the gobbler sound off from his roost in the swamp some 200 yards away. Only then did he sit up. The gobbler gobbled once more and Roy pinpointed his position. Roy's patience and perseverance in that very difficult situation had given us a perfect set up for the next morning's hunt.

An hour before dawn we were back at the exact spot where Roy had waited out the gobbler the evening before.

We had gone in early and without light to make certain that the old tom wouldn't detect our presence. Roy had picked out a fallen log as his ambush point. And he had decided to let me do the calling so that he could listen and learn from both me and the old tom.

I selected a calling spot in a thick clump of palmettos about 20 yards back of Roy so he would be in direct line between me and the roosting tom. At first light, I clucked softly on my box and both gobblers answered. One was in the area straight ahead that Roy had pinpointed the evening before, and the other was roosting another 300 or 400 yards to our left. The morning air was foggy and visibility was low. I waited and waited for another gobble, but heard only whippoorwills and owls.

Thirty minutes passed, and still no gobble. I knew the old toms should now be on the ground, so I eased out my tube and yelped softly. A few seconds later, I thought I heard the wings of a flying turkey, but I was buried so deep in that thick patch of palmettos that I wasn't sure. After a few more minutes, I again queried the foggy air with a soft yelp. And ten minutes later I yelped again, and got no response.

Just as I was thinking about yelping once more, Roy's gun blasted and I jumped out of my hiding place. Roy was standing stone still and a big gobbler was racing away from him at not more than 30 yards range. "Shoot again!" I yelled, but there was no need. Roy moved a few steps forward and began yelling as only a man can when he finally bags his first gobbler. Only one gobbler a day can be taken in Florida, and Roy had killed the bird he shot at with a perfect clean neck shot. His trophy weighed 18 pounds and had a ten-inch beard. Roy's hard work, patience, and perseverance had finally overcome both his long string of bad luck and the heavy hunter competition on this trip. He was at last a full fledged turkey hunter—a fact which he again demonstrated when, a month later, he called up and bagged an even bigger gobbler in New York, his home state.

LESSON #9: *Sharpen Up Your Turkey Calling By Practicing On Live Birds.* The most valuable lesson a man can learn from turkeys is how to call with more realism. No hunter can have real confidence in his spring turkey calling until he actually *hears* an old gobbler responding to his call, then *sees* the old monarch in full strut come to it.

Listening to other hunters call as well as listening to recordings of turkey talk are excellent ways to learn the mechanics of calling—and turkeys can be called up with no more practice than this. But practicing with *real live* turkeys will naturally increase the realism of a hunter's calls and up his chances for scoring. Unfortunately, it's difficult for most hunters to find live birds, either wild or domestic, to practice with.

As previously indicated, I was visiting recently with Joe Meeks at his Tellico Junction Hunting Preserve—and our specific objective was to develop a practical solution to this problem. Both Joe and I are very excited about the ideas we came up with. Our plan starts off with this premise: there are thousands of turkey hunters across the country who need a convenient place to go to where they can practice calling live turkeys and there are hundreds of shooting preserves scattered across the country which have or could have live wild birds for hunters to practice with. Why shouldn't these strategically located shooting preserves offer both gun and bowhunters practice and instruction in calling turkeys as an adjunct to their regular hunting programs? Wouldn't such a program of instruction solve the most acute problem now faced by turkey hunters—and couldn't preserve managers find a way to make it profitable?

Although preserve birds are pen-raised, they come from wild turkey stock and their talking habits and the tone of their calls resemble those of native wild birds. And, as my previously cited hunt with Joe indicates, after an old pen-raised gobbler has been in the woods for a few weeks, he can be just as tough and as much fun to call in as one hatched out and raised in the woods.

Even more exciting is the fact that pen-raised gobblers, like most wild ones, usually begin gobbling well ahead of hunting seasons and continue their gobbling well into the summer months, long after spring hunting seasons are over.

Since preserve hunting is allowed the year around or most of the year in most states, if spring gobbler calling practice was available at shooting preserves, hunters could take advantage of it for a full five or six months each year. And they could practice fall calls the rest of the year.

Joe is researching such a program and it is hoped that other shooting preserves across the country will do the same. These could be its main features:

(1) Turkeys of different sexes and age groups could be isolated in pens so that hunters could listen to the birds and learn their various calls and how to duplicate them. This should enable hunters to talk to real hens until they sound like them—then actually watch the reactions of old gobblers to their calls. When they are able to hit exactly the right notes that send an old tom into a full strut and a fit of gobbling, hunters would *know* they've mastered the *right* call.

(2) Actual hunting and field practice could begin as soon as hunters feel they've developed a satisfactory proficiency by practicing with the penned birds. Hunters could then be accompanied in the field by a guide who is also a proficient turkey caller. The guide could act as an instructor in tactics as well as calling until the big moment finally arrives and the hunter calls in and bags his own gobbler.

If the preserve nearest you is not yet offering this kind of instruction, why not suggest such a program and help sparkplug its immediate implementation? This could give you and other hunters in your area the chance to practice with the *real* thing—and on year-around or nearly year-around basis. There could be no better way to learn turkey hunting's most important lesson—how to talk turkey the way a real turkey talks.

CHAPTER 11

Saga Of A Two-Bearded Florida Gobbler

This strange tale sums up the mystique and manner of spring gobbler hunting—the sport I love above all others. You may find it hard to believe—not only because its main character was twin-bearded and finally outwitted in a most unorthodox manner, but because his every gobble was stranger than fiction in both composition and tone. In all my years of turkey hunting, I have never heard a thunder of passion resembling the one emitted by this old king of a Florida swamp. His totally unique explosion of unrequited love rang in my ears at least a hundred times. Otherwise, I wouldn't have believed that any gobbler was capable of producing such a call either. But the gobbler was real, his strange gobble was real, and this story is true.

I

"GOBBLE-OBBLE-OBBLE-OBBLE! GOBBLE-OBBLE-OBBLE-OBBLE! WO-WO-Wo-Wo-wo-wo!" I nearly fell off the decaying log. Sweet dizzying heat shot through me from head to toe. It was the old swamp gobbler I was after all right! Praise the Lord!

Again, "GOBBLE-OBBLE-OBBLE-OBBLE! GOBBLE-OBBLE-OBBLE-OBBLE! WO-WO-Wo-Wo-wo-wo!" What a wild—strange, even eerie—rattle and *wail* of ecstacy. It could be coming from no other living thing except the old swamp king I had first heard the day before. For long moments, I sat in reverent awe and listened to that spellbinding music which no man may have ever heard before—and one which no man may ever hear again. *Every* stirring run was a long four-syllable double-gobble followed by those rich, wailing, quavering, "WO-WO-Wo-Wo-wo-wo's" gradually decreasing in pleading intensity.

The incredible gobbling and wailing was stranger still because it was splitting the air almost continuously—and at 4 o'clock in the afternoon! And it was *not* coming from deep in the shaded swamp where the old tom had gobbled three times at dawn the morning before. Instead, it was echoing from a long palmetto-studded ridge fringing the swamp not a half-mile ahead of where I had parked the truck!

I was glad that afternoon hunting was not permitted in Florida. Instead of quickly calling up this magnificent adversary, I could now follow—and relish his every strange call as long as he would gobble. And with luck, I might roost him for the next morning's hunt.

I eased out of the dark wet swamp into the bright dry palmettos a few hundred yards from the weird rattling. I was almost blinded by the brilliant new world of intense sunlight, glittering greens, and azure sky. And I remained dizzy with excitement, for the old sultan, prancing and strutting somewhere in a sun-drenched clearing ahead, continued to boom out his fierce love growls followed by those passionate pleading wails. This had to be not only the strangest gobble I had ever heard, but also the hottest gobbler! This was one old bird I was *going* to roost—come hell or high water—and both *did* come before our final rendezvous.

A few minutes after six, nearly two hours before dark, the old tom began moving toward his roosting area, still gob-

This is typical Florida gobbler country where gobbles and wails can still be heard by hardworking hunters.

bling and wailing with almost every step. This made him easy to track. But his course seemed carefully designed to pass through, under, or over every possible obstacle which could stop or discourage a pursuing predator like me. First, the old bird zigzagged for nearly an hour through the tallest and thickest walls of palmettos and briar patches on top of the ridge. Trailing some 400 or 500 yards behind, and with sweat from the 90° heat almost blinding me, I followed in dense cover often higher than my head, while thorns punctured and scraped my legs.

Finally, the old gobbler's course left the open ridge and entered the swamp a good mile from the truck. There, in a mud hole at the base of the first cypress, he left his gigantic three-pronged prints to tantalize me more. This was a critical moment. I had to be able to return to this exact spot well

before light the next morning—and I had to be able to track
the gobbler on in to his roost. I took inventory of marking
materials in my pocket. I had a half-dozen sheets of white
Kleenex, a map, and an empty cigarette package. I stuck the
cigarette package on a small branch over the tracks at eye
level, and hoped to use small pieces of the Kleenex to mark
the gobbler's trail on in to his roost—then to use pieces of
the map later to mark my trail back to the truck.

The old tom moved on into the dark swamp continuing
to gobble and wail almost incessantly. I followed, sloshing
through ankle-to-knee-deep mud and crawling through tangles
of brush and foot-grabbing cypress roots and knees. Suddenly my way was blocked by a bog hole and switchgrass
hell too deep and thick to penetrate. The cagy old tom had
flown across it. That beautiful gobbler music was fading. I
had to hurry. Rushing and no longer worrying about my noisy
sloshing, I finally found a way to circle the pond in less than
waist-deep mud and water. With firmer footing I began to
move faster and to close on the wailing gobbler. It occurred
to me that this tropical mud and water world had to have
its share of moccasins, so I followed my usual strategy; I reminded myself that the prize was worth the risk, then kept
moving, and didn't look down.

The gobbler finally crossed the swamp, and I followed
him to the edge of a dry hardwood and palm hammock where
owls were beginning to moan from almost every giant oak
tree. I lay on the hard dry ground to catch my breath, and
listened to a symphony which can be heard only as a full
moon creeps up on a still Southern swamp in March. Every
male creature in the hammock, and in the mud and water
around it, was vocalizing his breast-busting love pains. Bull
'gators grunted like bass drums. Heron, egret, and limpkin
cocks joined in with their rasping barks of passion. And
against this background, scores of flutey and oboe-like owls
tried to play the lead. But each throbbing crescendo was
drowned completely out by the king of the swamp himself:
"GOBBLE-OBBLE-OBBLE-OBBLE! WO-WO-Wo-Wo-wo-
wo!" Nothing in this crowded swamp world was a match for
this mighty and aggressive gobbler—and he was proving it.

Oh, how rare and sweet it is to roost any gobbler. And roosting this old wailing sultan was a dream I hardly dared to dream—even now that I was so very close. As the sun died behind me, the full moon popped up in front—and the noise of the gobbler moved down the hammock to my left. The ground was now dark enough to close to 200 yards. I heard the gobbler flush—and against the last pinkness in the western sky, I watched his blur stop on a shaking cypress limb. Grinning like a swamp ghost, I eased a few yards closer.

The old tom was roosting in the center of a small dry pond just off the hammock edge. Against the darkening sky I watched him walk the limb searching for danger below with his long warty periscope. Satisfied that all was well, he then began to strut and gobble and wail again. Careful not to crack a single twig, I backed into the hammock once more and chose my calling spot for in the morning. The log was comfortable, and a full 200 yards from the roosting monarch, as it had to be. It lay within a few yards of the exact route the old tom had used to go to roost, and which he could be called back along most easily. And finally, the log was completely encircled by a thin veil of brush which would break up my profile, but which I could see and shoot through.

I sat down on the log and double-checked the brush for concealment and easy gun swing. The calling position was perfect! Impaling my last piece of Kleenex high on a point of brush, I headed for the truck with those beautiful wailing gobbles fading behind me.

Bright moonlight served as my flashlight which I had foolishly left in the truck. One by one I found the markers leading back to the cigarette package at the edge of the palmetto ridge. Locating the truck was more difficult, but I finally spotted it just before midnight—and just as I was running out of markers made of the map.

II

What a night of jubilant reminiscing and planning! The usually dim lights of the camper glowed and sparkled like great bonfires. My mind did flips re-sipping, again and again, every one of those thundering double-gobbles and amazing quavering wails. And a hundred times, I re-roosted the old black warrior against the pink sky—and watched him strut like a tight-rope walker on that wisp of a cypress limb. My hat was off to Florida wildlife managers who had given me this great moment in hunting.

For a second I panicked! Was I sure I could find my way back to the spot where the old gobbler had entered the swamp? The palmettos were thick and those pieces of map were mighty small. I grabbed my flashlight and a roll of white toilet tissue. Winding back across the ridge, I re-marked every ten feet of the twisting trail to the swamp edge and re-turned to the camper once more.

Dinner NOW! And only the best would do on this mo-mentous occasion. I made hot coffee and opened royal cans of chili verde and spinach. And I consumed the steaming after-midnight hunter's brew patting myself on the back. One brilliant and tough gamble had put me in this gobbler hunter's heaven. I had passed up several areas where I knew there were turkeys in this popular public hunting area because I knew there would be heavy hunter competition there. Instead, I had plowed into this rugged and hellacious swamp country— and on the one jeep trail I had found with no fresh tire tracks. And the gamble had paid off. At least, it had so far. I had heard no other vehicle as I listened to that long afternoon of sweet gobbler thunder.

Plan! Plan! Plan! I had to be completely ready for that great duel in the morning! I laid out a new set of noiseless cotton camouflage coveralls, still new, unfaded, and dark like the swamp where I would wait for the gobbler. Beside the coveralls and upside down, I placed my camouflage vinyl-covered cap through which no mosquito could drill. In the cap would go those items which would be critical and essential the next morning. In it I placed the can of "OFF" with which I would spray myself before dressing—and the tubes of camouflage grease paints I would use to mask my face and hands.

I would carry nothing which could rattle away my pres-

ence as I entered the old gobbler's domain and made my final
swing at him. In the cap, I placed the only three shells which
would go with me and my trusty old 1100—one #6 and two
#2's. I stowed all other shells in a cabinet drawer, along
with my watch, change, and even my old compass which now
rattled a bit. It was hard, but I had to do it. Even my trusty
old box which I usually clucked with went into storage in the
drawer, too. Only my completely silent waterproof and reliable old-hen and young-hen tube calls would go with me on
this duel of duels. These went in the cap, too, along with
my small pocketknife, wrapped in toilet tissue, and my wallet
with license.

My arsenal was ready—with one all-important exception.
Thank God for that new gum-grabbing plastic Polident! As I
laid out a tube, I toasted it, "Here's to you, baby. Tomorrow
morning when that old mouth tube must be held steady and
true—*you* will be the most important thing in the world!"

Polident—boy, I'd come a long way down the old turkey
hunting trail! And I wouldn't have traded a frustrating spine-
tingling moment of it for anything else. Even those old days
before I learned to call and to appreciate fitting rules for
dueling a majestic gobbler were great. Had this moment
been mine *then*, all my planning would have been directed at
sneaking under the old tom's roost tree and shooting him out
at the first legal early-morning moment. And I might well
have made the grade.

But now the duel was a far better one because it would
take both skill and luck to win. I had the gun, but all other
odds were shaded in favor of the gobbler. Lurking on that
log at daybreak, I would know the old gobbler's location and
he wouldn't know mine. But my yelps could only approximate
those of a hen, and a real hen might easily be waiting in
another direction to lure him away from me. I would be
camouflaged, still and hidden. But his eyesight was ten times
better than mine. I would have to gamble on snakebite as he
perched safely on that cypress limb. And as he flew and
walked protected by feathered armor, I would have to endure
attack by thousands of mosquitos without moving a muscle.

And to win, I would have to force myself to call sparingly

—just enough to let him *think* I was probably a hen, but not enough to let him *know* I wasn't one. And if he came tiptoeing in, long after his last gobble, I would have to force myself *to remain absolutely frozen, never turning my head to look for him.* I would have to sense when he was in shooting range—or hear him there—or *glimpse* the movement of his white head in that limited area where my eyes were preset. And then, I would be unable to gamble raising my gun until I could see his head disappear behind a tree or bush, or behind his strutting tail. Even then, I could squeeze off *only* if I got a clear shot at his vulnerable head and neck.

All these things I would have to do if the old tom came tiptoeing in the most usual manner—but this was a most unusual old gobbler. I wondered what kind of situation—and what kind of duel—the morning would really bring.

Planning complete. Clock reading three. Alarm set at five —and *ON*. Lights out. "GOBBLE-OBBLE-OBBLE-OBBLE! WO-WO-Wo-Wo-wo-wo!" Again, chills started running up and down my spine. "You shouldn't have let me roost you, old gobbler. To heck with the odds! If I don't take you in the morning, I'm the world's worst turkey hunter."

III

Big Florida lightning bugs snapped on and off like neon signs. And armadillos or wild hogs were busting palmettos ahead. While still far out of the gobbler's hearing, I loaded my gun. The full moon was still barely up and I was able to follow the markers without the flashlight. I left the ridge and moved through the swamp and down the hammock a slow inch at a time—for there was no way I was going to give my approach away to the roosting gobbler. I found the last marker and the black outline of the log and settled on it. I knew I was a full hour early, but on this momentous morning I wanted every advantage I could get. I waited without smoking and prayed I wouldn't cough.

The giant hammock hardwoods were already fully leafed by the early spring, and only a few patches of golden light twinkled through the thick black umbrella overhead. The woods were ominously silent. Only the occasional cry of a lonesome whippoorwill and chugging frogs broke the stillness. The gobbler, the owl, the egrets, and the herons were now resting and restoring energy for their next love performance which would begin near dawn. Even the big swarms of mosquitos were delaying their strike until first light.

Suddenly, my heart almost stopped! I could hear a Jeep grinding through mud far across the swamp. Was some other hunter coming in from the other side of the roosting gobbler, along some dim trail I didn't know existed? How many times such interference had ruined my best laid plans. It *couldn't* happen this time. This was such a special and private duel, fate *had* to honor it. The grinding finally stopped, I hoped further from this sacred combat area than it sounded.

As I waited for the first fingers of the hiding sun to blush the eastern sky, I watched great bronze gobblers from the past go strutting by in all their glory before my still un-believing eyes—and I listened to them shatter the woods with their thundering gobbles, again and again. But the gobbler I saw and heard most often was strutting against a pink sky on a wisp of cypress limb, and double-gobbling and *wailing* like none other I had ever heard. Even if I never saw or heard him again, this old swamp king would always be my gobbler of gobblers. But I hoped for a real rendezvous with him within the hour.

Dawn came in its usual miraculous way. One by one, stars flicked out in the east and were replaced by a sweep of slowly expanding grays and silvers. Hazy silhouettes turned into naked cypress trees—and into tall palms and gnarled hard-woods wearing thick umbrellas of leafy greens and drapes of spanish moss. The sky pinkened, and 'gators began booming in earnest—and the song of owls and pond birds slowly cres-cendoed to almost deafening proportions. *But not a solitary sound came from the old gobbler.* I began to sweat. Had he moved to another far-distant roost tree in the middle of the moonlit night? Had a wildcat or another approaching hunter spooked him? I waited. There was no need to hoot to try to make him gobble, for a hundred real owls were already hooting in concert.

Suddenly, "GOBBLE-OBBLE-OBBLE-OBBLE! WO-WO-Wo-Wo-wo-wo!" Excitement drilled me to the marrow! Combat was joined! The duel was on! I eased the safety off and the old hen tube from my pocket. That cagy old tom would get only one soft cluck while he was still in the tree. This would tell him exactly where I was, but not exactly what kind of turkey I was. It would start him thinking in my direction.

At that moment, a *man-made* gobble rang out from the other side of the old tom's roosting spot! Some naive hunter had come in and was trying to call up the wisest male bird in the world by *gobbling with a box!* Unless I worked fast, this hunter would probably do even worse—walk under the old tom and spook him out of the country. So, I threw caution to the winds, mouthed the tube and clucked twice, loudly and in rapid succession. And I followed the clucks with a long run of pleading yelps. Then I prayed I had sounded enough like a real hen.

I had. But the old tom was wary after hearing that phony gobble. Instead of flying down and walking to me, he flew straight to a treetop high above my head. Although I was looking up when he lit, I couldn't see him through the heavy umbrella of leaves and spanish moss. But I knew *he* knew exactly the patch of brush I was hiding in, and that his radar eyes were peering straight down into it.

To make matters worse, when I heard the old tom flying I had automatically come to a half-standing position with my heavy gun in my left hand and the call in my right. I was frozen in this awkward position, knowing that my slightest movement would spook the gobbler. What a ridiculous situation to get caught in. What a helpless feeling! Hunters as well as the hunted learn to make no move unless it is carefully calculated to improve a tense and critical predicament. What could I do but continue to look up and hope the old tom would move first and give his position away to me?

My eyes x-rayed every inch of foliage they could see without moving, over and over again. By now, I had determined that the treetops were so high and the foliage so thick, I wouldn't shoot at the tom even if I could make out his position. *It would be criminal to risk wounding and losing this majestic bird.* If I could remain frozen long enough, he might fly down within sure gun range, or to another not-too-distant area where I might have a chance to call him up later.

The man-made gobbling moved to my left. It shattered the air every five or ten minutes and was getting closer. A full thirty minutes ticked by, and with every tick the swarming mosquitos nailed me in spots where my repellent was wearing thin. My gun began to feel as if it weighed a hundred pounds —and my half-crouched body was now almost paralyzed.

Suddenly, out of the corner of my eye, I saw the hunter circling toward me, obviously in plain sight of the old gobbler! Young and tall, in blue jeans and without face or hand camouflage, he stopped in a bush about 100 yards to my left and continued to shake his noisy box at five or ten minute intervals. He even pulled out a sandwich and ate it! The sharp old tom must have known that this amusing spectacle posed no threat to him, for he continued to perch still and silent in the lofty tree above.

More long minutes ticked by and I died a thousand deaths. Finally, the hunter got up and moved within 30 yards. He finally made out my crouched form and painted face—and did a double-take. When his shock subsided, he must have thought I had seen a gobbler in the direction I was facing and that he had come from, for he began rapidly backtracking his own trail!

At this point, I was unable to remain in my crouched position any longer. I had to take the long gamble that the old tom, distracted by the other hunter, would also let me move away from him without spooking. I began walking slowly and in an unconcerned manner in the opposite direction. The old tom must have been so fascinated by watching *two* nuts walking away from his tree, that he forgot all natural caution. Miraculously, he stayed on the limb!

The moment I knew I was completely out of sight and hearing of the old gobbler, I stopped and took inventory of the situation. When the gobbler did decide to fly down, he certainly wouldn't fly south, the direction he had seen me departing. He wouldn't fly north, the direction he had seen the other hunter head. And, because of the human activity he had seen, it was unlikely that he would fly west to the open palmetto ridge. If I called him in at all that day, which was exceedingly unlikely, it would have to be to the east where he had not seen hunters and where cover was plentiful. I turned in that direction and found the going remarkably easy, for another high dry hammock extended in that direction.

IV

I reached a fairly open hardwood flat some 400 yards from the gobbler's position. There, in a pile of fallen logs, I made my stand. I figured my odds for calling in the old tom were now no better than 50 to 1—but if the woods ever quieted down, I could try. How great it was when that man-made gobbling finally ceased! I gave the old tom another half-hour to quit chuckling and perhaps to settle down to thoughts of love. The sun was now burning down from mid-morning high. All other swamp and hammock creatures had completed their lovemaking and were quiet again. I could only hope against hope that the old gobbler was still lusty.

I started to reach for my trusty old-hen tube once again. Then I realized this could be sheer folly. The old tom had already heard the coarse notes of this call and had flown to the tree above their source only to discover a hunter instead of a hen below. So, instead, I raised the young-hen tube to my lips and sent a fine, pleading, high-pitched "Kee-oak! Kee-oak! Kee-oak!" in the direction of the gobbler's tree.

Instantly, I heard another gobbler hunting miracle! The old sultan thundered back with that beautiful double-gobble and wail. What had this old hunter done to deserve a heavenly second chance like this? But I still couldn't believe it was possible to actually call that old bird in after all the human activity he had seen under his tree that long morning.

I was almost afraid of giving myself away as a phony hen by calling again. But I decided to risk one more call. I cupped the tube tightly in my hands, turned down and away from the gobbler—and as soft as I could blow, I sent two more fine yelps into the ground. Their delicate echoes were picked up by razor-sharp ears in that tree a good 400 yards

away! "GOBBLE-OBBLE-OBBLE-OBBLE! GOBBLE-OB-
BLE-OBBLE-OBBLE! WO-WO-Wo-Wo-wo-wo!" With trem-
bling fingers, I put the call in my pocket, then picked up my
gun. Now, the old gobbler knew exactly the pile of logs I
was hiding in—and he thought I was a real hen.

In all my years of turkey hunting, I haven't had a dozen
gobblers fly all the way in to me. But it happened a second
time that morning. I heard the distant "Puff-puff-puff-puff" of
rapid wing beats—then glimpsed a blur gliding downward

Old Osceola had razor-sharp spurs nearly an inch and a half long.

To get to my two-bearded gobbler, I had to wade through swamps like these.

through the treetops. Over my gun barrel, I watched the blur grow larger and larger—then made out cupped wings and heard their whistling against the still air. My heart beat like a rock hammer. And I asked my hands to quit shaking.

Then a sky full of vertical wings were braking a monstrous body at point-blank range—then gently lowering the great bronze form those last few inches in a spray of dust and leaves. Somehow, I managed to focus on the long outstretched neck and to squeeze off on its blue and white tip. The echoes of my gun shot faded in the distance. My mind slowly cleared. The impossible had happened! I had finally won my finest duel—and in the face of almost unbelievable odds.

Today, my respected opponent, which weighed seventeen

My old gobbler had twin 10-inch beards.

pounds, stands in the center of my den in full and honorable mount. His *two* ten-inch *twin* beards, growing from two distinct stubs an inch apart, are unique badges of honor which hunters will admire for years to come. He stands on pencil-thin and bright-red legs with sharp spurs, curved and shiny black, and more than an inch long. His powerful streamlined body is shadowy dark like the swamps he ruled. His feathers are far less barred than those of his cousin, the Eastern turkey. And under his handsome creamy-white crown, his leathery cheeks and neck skin are dark slate blue with only tiny tips of red on the caruncle points. These features mark him as a pure-blooded Florida turkey, or *Meleagris gallopavo osceola*— the only such trophy I have ever been privileged to take. All others I've taken in Florida were Eastern turkeys.

As I admire my handsome opponent, as I do on so many long and special evenings, I'm always doubly glad that the peak of the mating season had passed when I finally brought him gliding in. He had undoubtedly impregnated every hen in the area. In a couple of springs, I can hope that his identical offspring is assuming command of his dark swamps, his lonesome hardwood hammocks, and his emerald palmetto-studded ridge. And I can hope that some fortunate hunter will also hear that strange and beautiful "GOBBLE-OBBLE-OBBLE-OBBLE! GOBBLE-OBBLE-OBBLE-OBBLE! WO-WO-Wo-Wo-wo-wo!"—and perhaps also go home with a pure-blooded Osceola gobbler with two beards.

CHAPTER 12

How To Call So
Fall Turkeys Hunt *You*

Just as the sky turned pink, I heard the swish of great wings, and saw two gobblers flying down the ridgetop in my direction. I knew they had been spooked off their roost by another hunter. Just before reaching my position, the birds split. One glided down the ridge to the thick bottom below, and the other sailed on past just out of gun range and lit on the ridgetop some 300 yards beyond.

Taking advantage of the dim light, I moved to a small clearing on a direct line between the two spots where the old gobblers had landed. I found a comfortable log with a pine behind it I could lean against and with enough scrub oak in front of it to break up my silhouette. I could see the clearing well enough to shoot—and that's where I intended to kill one of the old toms, an "odd" couple batching it together in this rugged section of New Mexico's Lincoln National Forest.

I waited an hour before picking up my call, then I imposed a coarse "Where-are-you?" cluck on the mountain stillness. Almost immediately, the gobbler below answered with an identical cluck. I answered with two more loud clucks, and the gobbler clucked back. Now sure that I was his buddy, the old bird headed straight to me, clucking once or twice at three or four minute intervals. I answered every second or third of his clucks with a similar one.

Suddenly, leaves rustled on the downhill edge of the clearing, and I saw the silhouette of the old Merriam standing with his head behind a ponderosa trunk. I eased my gun to the shoulder and waited. Then the awe-inspiring statue of the old monarch stepped out into the sunlit clearing. His long neck and red warty head formed a prying periscope looking directly away from me.

An instant before I began the trigger pull, the second mighty gobbler, looking like a twin to the first, also stepped into the clearing from the uphill side! He had come without saying a word. I hesitated a second, trying to decide which mammoth bird was the better trophy—and this delay almost cost me a shot. The second gobbler suddenly made me out, boomed out a sharp alarm putt, and both gobblers began running head down for oak brush. I just managed to swing the gun barrel in front of the first gobbler before he disappeared. But my pattern of #6's bracketed his head and neck —and one of my finest Merriams, a twenty-pounder, was mine.

I bagged that beautiful gobbler not because I hunted him, but because I made *him hunt me.* This tactic is by far the surest and easiest way to bag any turkey in the fall—whether you're hunting western Merriams, southwestern Rio Grandes, or Eastern or Florida turkeys. It also illustrates that fall turkey hunting is very different from spring turkey hunting. *The fall habits of turkeys are completely different from their spring habits just discussed—and an entirely different set of tactics is required to hunt fall turkeys successfully.*

The purpose of this chapter is to summarize those very different techniques which are required to call up both old gobblers and young turkeys in the fall. Before proceeding with this main task, let's take a quick look at six important tips on selecting a good fall turkey hunting area and scouting it properly.

TIPS ON SELECTING AND SCOUTING A
FALL HUNTING AREA

1. *Select A Hunting Area With A Good Turkey Popu-lation.* Most state game and fish agencies publish turkey harvest figures showing counties or wildlife management areas which produced the most birds during the previous year. These will probably be the best areas to hunt in the approaching fall, too. Secure this information along with area maps and hunting regulations. If possible, also check with a local conservation officer, forest ranger, sporting goods store, or old turkey hunter in each promising area for information on the current hunting outlook. After a thorough evaluation of this information, decide on the area you wish to hunt.

2. *Plan To Scout And Hunt At Least A Week.* To have any substantial probability of adequately scouting an area and bagging a fall turkey, you'll need this much time. If possible, allocate consecutive days for scouting and hunting, instead of scheduling several weekend-only trips. Your odds for bagging a turkey will be much higher on weekdays because hunting pressure is lightest then. And reading sign or spotting birds for several days in a row will give you the best chance for forecasting the movement of birds and getting into position to bag one.

3. *When You Reach Your Hunting Area, Begin An All-Out Search For Turkey Tracks.* Drive roads and walk trails, paying particular attention to sandy and muddy areas. Remember if only gobblers or "bearded" birds are legal game, numerous small tracks don't mean a thing in the fall. At this time of the year, these merely indicate the presence of hens and young birds. Instead, continue your search until you find *big* tracks—either single big tracks or big tracks made by a few birds. Only these will confirm that you're in fall gobbler country.

4. *As You Search For Tracks, Also Keep A Sharp Lookout For Droppings And For Bare Spots In Leaves Which Have Been Scratched Out By Turkeys Looking For Food.* Big gobbler tracks may be spotted in a scratched area. Large round droppings usually are produced by old gobblers, whereas

longer, slimmer droppings are usually dropped by hens and young birds.

5. *As You Search, Also Look For Roost Areas.* These can be identified by droppings under trees, by scarred limbs above and sometimes by loose feathers lying about. Merriam and Rio Grande turkeys are very prone to roost in large numbers and in the same spots for long periods of time. Therefore, their roosts are often easy to find. Eastern turkeys are not this cooperative, but it is possible to locate their roosts, too—especially during the early season days before they're spooked by hunters.

6. *If You Plan To Camp In Your Hunting Area, Camp Within Walking Distance Of The Freshest And Most Significant Sign You Find*—but not so close that your camp noises will spook turkeys out of that area or make them deviate from their normal movement patterns.

HOW TO GET HUNTED BY AN OLD GOBBLER

Habits of the Old Gobbler

In the fall, old gobblers are almost always confirmed bachelors. They seldom associate with flocks of hens and young birds, as they do in the spring; that is, they don't unless their paths happen to cross in feeding areas. And they will show no interest whatsoever in any hen call at this time of the year. A few old gobblers batch it alone, or with a group of several other old gobblers; but most have one other close "buddy" or perhaps two. As the preceding account of my New Mexico hunt indicated, these "odd" couples or trios form a strong bond of friendship. They are almost inseparable, roosting together, feeding together, and nooning together. And when they split up, you may be sure they will attempt to rendezvous as soon as they think it's safe. For this reason, the best way to make an old gobbler hunt you is to spook him away from his buddies—then, at the right time, to use a *gobbler* call to make him think you're one of his equally lonesome pals.

Calls for Fall Hunting

The same "clucks" you use for spring hunting will also work in the fall. But you'll also need to learn two other important calls for fall hunting: the gobbler's "whine," the "kee-kee" run of the young turkey, which can be made with any caller except the box. These calls will be described in detail in the text which follows.

How to Work an Old Gobbler Roost Area

If you know where one or more old gobblers are roosting, either by finding their fresh droppings under a tree or by being lucky enough to see or hear them fly up at dusk, you have two promising courses of action for the next morning's hunt. If you saw only one gobbler fly up, there's a good chance that the old toms were split up that afternoon and that this bird's buddy or buddies are roosting elsewhere. In this case, easing quietly to the edge of the nearest clearing to the roost tree, hiding good until daylight, then *clucking* softly when the sun is almost up, may bring him flying straight to you.

On the other hand, if you know or believe there are two or more gobblers roosting in the *same* area, your chances of calling them off the roost are mighty slim. If the "odd" couple or trio is together, the birds usually will pay no attention to the call of another gobbler. In this instance, it is better to move in before daylight and to position yourself as close to the roost as possible. Then, when it's light enough to see well, you may be in shooting range of a bird; if not, you should at least have a good chance of jumping out of your hiding place and of scattering the birds so you'll have a chance to call one back later.

How to Scatter Feeding Gobblers

If you ease through the woods quietly, it is also possible to top a ridge and spot a flock of old acorn-feeding gobblers, or to spot a flock feeding on green plants or grasshoppers in an open meadow or clearing. If possible, use available cover to sneak as close as possible to the birds, then scatter them by rushing straight at them and shouting or shooting your gun. Of course, this action assumes that you are interested in *calling* one of the old toms up. It is sometimes possible to stalk turkeys successfully using tactics detailed in the next chapter. However, if a stalk fails, the old toms will usually spook and run off together and you'll then lose any chance of calling one up later.

In states where it's legal, the use of turkey dogs is the easiest of all means for locating and scattering any flock of fall turkeys. Do you have a hardheaded pointer with excess speed and spirit—one that never holds, runs up every bird he smells or sees and even barks when the birds flush? If so, don't despair. Your "world's worst" bird dog may be the "world's best" turkey dog! According to Tom Rodgers, these are exactly the characteristics that make a good turkey dog. Tom and a small band of Virginia hunters are trying to revive the ancient and once highly respected sport of using dogs to trail and flush fall turkeys. This type of hunting requires dogs that will trail turkeys at top speed, rush and bust up a flock when they overtake it and bark when the birds scatter so the hunter will know where to sit down and attempt to call the birds back. The ideal turkey dog will then lie motionless by his master's side until a turkey is called in and bagged. But if your dog won't do this, you still have no big problem. Just do as Tom has had to do so far: take your dog back to the car before you begin calling. Before you try Old Rover on turkeys, however, make sure the use of dogs for turkey hunting is legal in your hunting area.

How to Call Scattered Gobblers

Once you've scattered old gobblers by any means, your next step is to make one of them hunt you. This requires making him think you are one of his lonesome pals. This in turn requires calling from a *believable* position, at a *believable* time, and with *believable* calls. And, if you're hunting a cagy old tom, "believable" has to be *really* believable. A hunter can make mistakes in positioning himself and calling when hunting young turkeys, and often get away with them. But when hunting old fall toms, if the position you call from, the time you call, or the way you call does not closely simulate the natural actions of a real spooked and lonesome gobbler you'll be identified as a phoney every time.

The first decision you must make when you split up a flock of old gobblers is whether to call from the area the birds flushed from or from another area. If you're lucky enough to see two or more birds head in the same general direction and fan out a considerable distance apart before lighting, as my two New Mexico gobblers did, the best spot to call from is one about midway between where the birds lit and on a straight line between them. On the other hand, if you don't see the birds flush, or if you see the birds flush generally away from each other when spooked and you don't see them go down, it is usually best to call from the flushing site. If the terrain is mountainous or hilly, the best specific calling spot is one just *above* the spot the birds flushed from; for returning toms will usually circle uphill and around the flushing site, probably so they can see the area below and check it for danger. They can also hear your calls further if you call from a high point.

The second important step in making an old tom hunt you is to make no call for at least an hour after the birds are split up—and to remain on your stand for several hours before giving up. Unlike young birds, which sometimes come to a call within thirty minutes, old fall toms are far more cautious and usually wait at least an hour or two before attempting to rendezvous. Premature calling is likely to tip them off that you are not the real McCoy.

As already indicated, coarse clucks are most often used by old gobblers when attempting to rendezvous; therefore, this is also the best all-around call to use when attempting to call one of them up. If you can't make a coarse or low-pitched cluck on your soft caller, use the *gobbler* side of your box. If an old tom is a long way off, you may get a short gobble in first response to your clucks and a few yelps later on—but far more often, the gobbler will only cluck back or come to you without saying a word. As a general rule, it is best to cluck once or twice at about ten minute intervals, remaining still and always looking for that sly old bird that may come without answering. If you do get an answer of any kind, repeat the same call with the same tone. Remember, you're two old buddies, lonesome and wanting to get together—but also cautious. You'll hear this feeling in his clucks or yelps. Put the same feeling in yours—and he'll usually come.

How to Whine In an Old Gobbler

As already indicated, old long-bearded gobblers use calls intended only for the understanding and benefit of another

Old Merriam gobblers are easy to locate and call in when a fresh snow is on the ground.

gobbler. In addition to those frequent clucks and occasional gobbles and yelps already covered, they may also use a long whiney call. For the want of a better name, most hunters refer to it as the "wildcat" call, as it sounds similar to a call of this animal. This call opens additional possibilities for the fall gobbler hunter who learns to use it. It must be learned by hearing wild gobblers use it, or from an old turkey hunter who knows how to make it, or from a good turkey calling record, as domestic gobblers never use it. But wary old wild gobblers often use the whine at dawn, at dusk, and on moonlit nights. You should learn to use it to advantage, too.

Let's assume that you separated a flock of gobblers around 3 p.m. and stayed in your blind until dusk trying unsuccessfully to call one of them up. It is almost dark now and you hear two or three lonesome high-pitched whines coming from high up on a ridge-side above you. These calls are made by one of your gobblers telling the others where he is and where he is going to roost. Upon hearing the call, the other gobblers may fly immediately to the one calling if sufficient daylight remains or if it is a moonlit night. Most often, however, they will spot the location, but wait to fly there until the next morning. So, if you're in the whining gobbler's general location at daybreak and make this same call, one of the gobblers is very likely to fly to you. When using this call, always select an area, preferably an elevated point or ridge, with large trees, for at daylight, this call is always associated with a gobbler on a roost.

HOW TO GET HUNTED BY YOUNG TURKEYS

Why Either-Sex Seasons are Held

Young turkeys hatched the preceding spring are most numerous in the fall woods and are easiest to call up. And in states where "any turkey" seasons are still held, the hunter need have no compunction about shooting a young bird. Population trends are carefully studied by competent biologists and either-sex seasons are held only in areas that can sustain such hunting without harm to the turkey population as a whole.

Composition of the Fall Turkey Flock

Understanding the composition of a typical flock of fall turkeys is important in order to know how to hunt and call them. In the fall months, when most turkey seasons are held, a typical flock will consist of a mother hen and four to eight young birds, about half young gobblers and half young hens— or of several families like these which have banded together. Since the big majority of birds in these flocks are young birds, and since young birds are easiest to call up, they are ideal targets for new hunters. A clear understanding of the habits of the young hen and of the young gobbler are the most important considerations.

The Young Hen

In the fall of the year, the young hen is six to eight months old. She is now nearly the size of her mother but not nearly so wise or heavy. She is usually called a "young turkey," a "turkey of the year," a "ginny," or "yearling." She is by nature very wild, but more trusting and less suspicious than her brothers. When flushed or separated, she uses her voice more frequently than any other class of turkeys and is the easiest to call by a hunter. Just like young girls, "she talks more than anybody else." Her calling sounds are high pitched, fresh, snappy, thin, young—and are beautiful to hear. Her vocabulary normally consists of "Kee-Kee-Kee's" (to be described later) and sometimes "yelps" when lost, changing to "clucks" when she gets closer in.

When she sees something out of place and wants to call the attention of the other turkeys to it, she makes a continuous sounding "Purr" and every turkey head within hearing goes up high—looking. She uses the call as we would use "Caution," "Careful," or "Watch Out." Normally, her yelps are used for long distance work and are aimed to carry about 200 yards. However, she is capable of calling very loud to overcome greater distances or when the wind is blowing, but seldom tries to be heard too far. She is also capable of yelping very softly for shorter distances especially if the drove is accustomed to being flushed frequently. Under these conditions she may come to

your calling without uttering a sound. Her kee-kee run may
be classed as her way of crying or asking for the company of
another turkey—especially one of her same sex. So, it is a
well executed and similar version of the kee-kee run which
will most often call her in.

The Young Gobbler

Nature makes the young gobbler larger and heavier than
his sisters with much more proudness and vanity. She also
endowed him with cunningness and peculiar quirks that challenge all the faculties hunters possess. Perhaps keeping his
mouth shut and listening when others of his kind talk account
for the fact that so many young gobblers grow old. Unlike
his sisters, he has little or no trust, no curiosity, is very independent and suspicious of everything in the woods. Follow
in his tracks in the snow and you'll see where he suddenly
turned off the trail to bypass a stump, a large rock, or log
that he couldn't quite see behind.

He is a creature of few words but he means what he says
when he speaks. His sister may walk around the hill and call
three or four different times, but this fellow is more inclined
to bide his time, make one call and if he doesn't get some
response, keep quiet. He is more inclined to "look up" another gobbler or to find another turkey by following the habits
of the drove than to give his position away by calling.

When they do call in the fall, lost young gobblers may
use a kee-kee run, similar but a little richer and deeper than
that of their sisters. Or, they may use slightly coarser yelps
—or a combination of kee-kee runs and yelps. However, they
often seek and answer each other with clucks only. Regardless of their call, they use it sparingly and cautiously. Sharp
hunters take advantage of this trait of the young gobbler
by hiding well and by calling in the same manner.

How to Read the Flush or a Turkey Flock

A flock of young birds and their mother hens can be located and flushed by the same general methods discussed
earlier for locating and flushing a flock of old gobblers. When

The author called up these two fall hens with kee-kee runs and photographed them at ten-yard range.

any flush occurs, the hunter should try to answer three questions: (1) Were the birds actually separated? (2) How many were there? (3) What kind were they?

If the answer to the first question is "Yes, they flew away in different directions," your chances for calling one of the birds back to the flushing site are excellent. But if they all flew off in one direction so each could see the others in flight, they will land together or quickly assemble right after landing.

In this case, you know that none will return to the flushing site.

The answer to the second question "How many?" also determines your odds for success. The larger the flock, if separated, the better your chances are for calling one of the birds back; for when a large flock is flushed, only a few birds usually see the hunter, and the remainder will usually respond readily to a call.

The answer to the third question is also important. If the birds were old gobblers, as is often the case if the flock is very small, you'll know to use the old gobbler calling tactics discussed earlier. On the other hand, if you know the birds were hens and young birds, as is usually the case if the flock is large, you'll know to use young bird calling tactics. You may occasionally flush a flock of young gobblers or young hens that have wandered away from the main flock. It's important to learn how to identify both so that you'll know which call to use when you try to call them back. Remember, the hens are smaller, trimmer, and more brownish than black.

The time of the day you flush a flock is also significant, for it tells you the best time to begin your attempts to call the birds back in. Normally, if the birds are flushed soon after daylight, they will attempt to re-group in from thirty minutes to two hours. If separated later on in the morning, this time lapse may be as much as three or four hours. If flushed about noon, they will usually get together just before sundown. But, if flushed from midafternoon on, they will usually wait until dawn the next day to re-group.

How to Make a Good Blind

Since most fall turkeys are called up and bagged when attempting to re-group at the flushing site, this discussion of blinds will be confined to that situation. Most suggestions, however, also apply to selecting and constructing a turkey blind anywhere. First of all, the blind should be natural in appearance and blend with its surroundings. When locating it, also bear in mind that returning birds are most likely to walk back in from the same direction they flushed, and that they like to approach the site using an open area. So, it's best to select a blind site overlooking such an area, and one with the sun at your back, if possible.

An old stump, a large tree, or a large rock makes an ideal blind backrest, as it breaks up your silhouette and also protects your back from some rattle-brain who might sneak up on you as you call and end your turkey hunting for good. Make yourself a comfortable and low seat against the backrest. Then stick a row of green branches in the ground to form a broken semicircle some six to eight feet in front of your seat. On the inside of this cover, place another circle of thin branches between your seat and the outer circle. You can easily see out of this kind of blind, yet the turkey cannot easily see into it. And make as little noise as possible when building the blind.

In selecting the blind site, it is also important to stay a reasonable distance away from thick undergrowth. When lost turkeys get into a thicket they are hard to call out even though they may answer readily. And when you're calling close to a thicket, an approaching turkey may well fly up into a nearby tree to check the thicket for danger. It will usually sit there and cluck until it sees another turkey. When that turkey sees the one in the tree, it will sense danger and probably fly up, too. Then you'll have two turkeys in trees warning any other approaching turkey of danger. This undesirable situation can be licked in advance by keeping your blind at least 100 yards from thickets.

How to Call Scattered Young Birds

Now that you've flushed the flock, evaluated the flush, and constructed your blind, you're ready to reverse the hunting procedure. From now on, your plans will be aimed at making a young turkey hunt you. To do this successfully, you must assume the role of a turkey. You are no longer a man, but a young gobbler or a young hen. You're an actor and you must play the role with all the realism possible.

And now, your role is to sit stone-still and listen, for several hours if necessary. Be alert to all sounds in the woods, especially any which might indicate the approach of a turkey —like the chatter of a squirrel or the excited chirp of a jay, a cardinal, a crow, or a robin. If you hear such a possible tip-off, send out two questioning clucks: "Are you there? Are you there?" If you get no response, query the woods anyway at ten minute intervals; first, with the fine pleading kee-kee's of the young hen, then with the deeper kee-kee's of the lonesome young gobbler followed by a yelp or two.

If you hear a turkey, answer it immediately in the same tone and with the same feeling. When the turkey is still far out, answer its every call with one like it. As it gets closer in, answer every second or third of its calls—but don't remain quiet too long. If you do, the approaching turkey is likely to sense that danger has made you stop calling, and he'll be likely to quit calling and coming, too. Most often you'll get kee-kee runs and maybe yelps from your "brother" or "sister" until he or she gets in close—then, most likely, soft clucks. At this point, each cluck of your quarry should be answered with *one* or *two* soft clucks, just loud enough to be heard.

Remember, you're a turkey that just happened to reach the assembly point first. You are anxious to get with the other turkey, but somewhat confused because you can't see it. You're telling the approaching turkey that you need help to fix its position—and you're pleading with him to give it to you—but soft and cautiously. This feeling must be conveyed by your calls. Playing this role, getting this feeling into your calls, is the whole secret of successful turkey calling. The worst mistake you can make is to have so little confidence in your calling that you're afraid each call you make will be off-key. For if you have such fear, it will certainly be reflected in the feeling of your calls.

It is a mother hen which is most likely to give you trouble in playing your role as a young turkey trying to call another young turkey to you. She may fly back within 100 yards of you and begin a series of rapid yelps or clucks which will last for several minutes. And every young turkey hearing her will go straight to her. If you don't run her off immediately, she will have the whole flock assembled around her and they'll all be gone in short order. Or she may light in a tree several hundred yards from the flushing spot and begin her loud assembly calling—then fly to a tree further away, then another, all the while yelping or clucking. In minutes, she'll have all the young birds with her and be far away. There's little you can do about this situation except to look for a new flock to flush. Always remember that there's no way that you, or even another real hen, can compete with a noisy excited mother

To call a wary old fall gobbler in, both the position you call from and the time you call have to be really believable. Remember, you're an old tom trying to entice another old tom to come to you.

hen for the attention of her young birds. The young birds know their mother's voice as well as you know yours. This is true even though the mother hen doesn't know the individual voice of each of her poults.

Random Calling

The tactics for hunting both old gobblers and young birds just discussed were based primarily on locating and splitting a flock up; for this situation offers the most promise during the fall hunting season. However, there will be times when it's impossible to locate and flush a flock, especially during the latter days of the season. This is usually true because they have already been widely scattered by heavy and repeated hunting pressure. If you know you're in country occupied by turkeys and can't find a flock, you may be reasonably sure that scattered birds are around. You may also be sure that these birds are lonesome and looking for company. So, easing through the woods and calling like another lost turkey may still get you a bird.

It's good practice to ease along ridgetops or along other high ground, and to do your calling from high points where you will be heard for a considerable distance. Hide well at each good calling point and call for at least thirty minutes— at ten minute intervals—whether or not you get a reply. Often a lonesome, but scared lost turkey will come without saying a word. In areas where either-sex turkeys are legal, the pleading kee-kee run of the young hen is most apt to get a response. But don't hesitate to kee-kee or yelp like a lost young gobbler, or to cluck like a lost old gobbler, if the young hen calls bring no response. If you do get an answer, respond to it in exactly the same ways already recommended for calling up lost turkeys from a flock you have scattered.

HOW TO SHOOT A TURKEY

These brief tips should help bag your fall bird when you finally call it in:

1. Remain still and look only in the direction from which you believe a turkey is most likely to approach. Don't keep

turning your head and looking in other directions. Listen for a soft call or the rustle of leaves telling you a bird is approaching.

2. Have your shotgun loaded with #6's or #4's, pointed in the same direction and in an easy-to-reach position.

3. If you must call, make certain that your hand movements are minimal.

4. Watch for movement—not the still form of a turkey. When you spot movement and determine that it's made by a turkey, freeze and study the bird. If you're hunting a gobbler only area, identify the bird as legal as quickly as possible.

5. When the turkey's head disappears behind a tree or bush, ease your call down and pick up your gun. Wait until you are certain the turkey is in sure range—then, when its head again disappears from view, ease your gun to your shoulder and point it at the spot where the turkey is likely to emerge. When the turkey's head reappears, ease the bead just below it—and fire.

6. Aiming tactics with a bow are fully covered in Chapter 16.

HOW TO LEARN FALL TURKEY TALK

All tactics just discussed for fall hunting were based on the use of only four basic calls: the kee-kee run, the yelp, the cluck, and the whine or wildcat call. Of course, these calls should be varied as previously indicated, to fit the sex, age, and mood of the bird you're imitating. You can learn to make all these calls with Leon's suction-type caller, or with any other of the mouth-operated callers discussed in Chapter 2. And they can be made with a slate-type caller. A good caller can cluck, yelp and whine with a box caller, but most cannot make a believable kee-kee run with one.

All these calls can be learned in a reasonable time by listening to a good instructor or to a good recording of turkey

(Author's Note: The late Leon Johenning was one of the greatest turkey hunters of all time and inventor of the famous Leon Turkey Caller. Many of the tips summarized in this chapter are covered in great detail in Leon's book *The Turkey Hunter's Guide*. This classic, and Leon's caller and instructional records, are now being distributed by his wife and son through L.C.J. Manufacturing Co., 114 Randolph Street, Lexington, Va. 24450.)

calls, such as those also discussed in Chapter 2. It is usually most practical to start with a recording or instructor in order to learn what the basic calls sound like and how to produce them with the caller you intend to use. But to get that real live feeling in your calling, you should also work with live birds—either at a shooting preserve or at a nearby farm. Although domestic birds don't sound exactly like wild ones, for the purpose of practice, their calls are close enough to the real thing.

Your training program for fall calling should begin about the middle of summer as young turkeys will then be yelping, clucking, and kee-kee-ing. If possible, find a preserve manager or a farmer who is raising a drove with the old mother hen. Set up a short section of wire fence to make a circle, and in this enclosure place one of the young hens. As soon as the young bird settles down a bit, it will feel lost from the others and will begin to call. Listen intently to the way it calls

Leon Johenning's suction turkey caller is especially good for fall hunting.

and try to produce the same rhythm and timing with your breath and voice. No doubt the bird will yelp and kee-kee. You should practice these same calls with your lips until you can do a good imitation along with the turkey. Pay particular attention to what the bird is trying to convey in its voice. There are any number of feelings you can identify, such as: loneliness, excitement, alarm, anxiety, sadness, and distress. You should concentrate your attention on this young hen's calling until you know you can repeat the same tone, timing, and feeling of all her calls—automatically. For the next few days repeat the same process, but this time take your caller along. Sit down close to the calling bird and endeavor to duplicate its various calls and mannerisms. This same procedure should be repeated until you know the voice of a young hen and can duplicate it on your caller. Should you have access to a tape recorder, also record her calls for home practice.

After learning the hen calls, you should place a young gobbler, then an old one, in the enclosure and continue as before. With live birds to practice with, your calling will take on a *live* tone and meaning. You'll be talking turkey just as live turkeys talk in the fall.

If you live a long distance from a shooting preserve or farmer with live turkeys, at least scout your hunting area a few days before the season opens with caller and camera. Wild birds should be fairly easy to locate then, and listening to a flock and calling up even a single bird will give you valuable experience and confidence in your fall calling. Such a trip can also give you treasured photos and a lot of fun.

CHAPTER 13

How To Hunt Turkeys Without A Call

Several years ago I was gunning for springtime gobblers in the pine-and-oak studded mountains near Raton, New Mexico. This area probably is surpassed only by Wyoming's Black Hills as the best spot in the West for hunting the stately Merriam turkey. It was early morning on the second day of our hunt. I pleaded with my son Doug to stay with me on a choice stand overlooking a dusty clearing where numerous tracks and marks of drooping wings indicated recent strutting activity. "Nope, Dad," Doug whispered. "I got tired of sitting here yesterday. Today I'm going to try and *sneak up* on a gobbler. At least I'll see some new country that way!" Shaking my head, I watched Doug disappear into the early morning shadows.

I sat down on the same stump I had warmed so long the day before, pulled my camouflaged parka tightly around my already chilled torso, extracted my old box from my pocket, and began calling. That crazy kid of mine! Imagine his trying to *stalk* a gobbler.

As the sun poked through the pine tops, I was answered by the expected booming gobble just uphill from the clearing. In the next half hour, the old gobbler sounded off—twenty times, and the last gobble told me he was approaching the upper edge of the clearing. My goose pimples grew goose pimples. I emitted two more soft and seductive yelps, this time with my trusty tube, then picked up my gun.

Suddenly, the old Merriam stepped out into plain view. Although he was a good 100 yards away, I could see that both his huge belly and beard almost dragged the ground. Then my dreams were shattered. The big bird went into full strut as a half dozen hens materialized around him. Then he ambled off with the hens in spite of my pleading calls with both box and tube—and I saw him no more.

I returned to camp empty-handed for the second day in a row. Doug was already back and hanging from the game rack on our camp trailer was a 23-pound Merriam gobbler—one bigger than any I have ever killed in all my years of turkey hunting. I could hardly believe my eyes. Doug had not only racked up an almost unbelievable trophy—but he had done it *without* a call! And he rubbed it in. "Dad, why don't you throw those old fashioned calls away and get your gobbler the *easy* way?" Against my better judgment, I tried a stalk hunt too, right after lunch. And by 3 p.m. I, too, had a 19-pounder hanging up by Doug's turkey. And the following fall, using the stalk as our *only* hunting tactic, Doug and I both filled out with big toms on the first day of our hunt in the same area where it usually took us several days of hard calling to nail any turkey. I finally had to admit that it can sometimes pay to throw away the book and to hunt turkeys without a call.

All turkeys can be bagged without a call; however, Merriams in the more open West are by far the easiest to hunt in this manner. And any old tom is easiest to hunt without a call in the spring for two reasons. First, in the spring he spends a lot of time strutting and when doing so, he can often be spotted almost as easy as a neon sign. Second, an old love-lorn spring gobbler is preoccupied with affairs of the heart which dull, at least to some degree, his normal alertness and

Doug took this monster 23-pound Merriam by stalking him in the spring. He scores nearly every year and rarely uses a call.

caution—and this also gives the spring stalker some advantage. The two big toms which Doug and I nailed on our first spring no-call hunt were both in full strut the entire time we slipped up on them. The other two gobblers we clobbered the following fall were "singles" we slipped up on while they were nooning in pine shadows.

Yes, although most of us prefer to call our birds in, let's admit that a no-call gobbler hunt can pay off—in the spring or in the fall. Here are a few secrets for making them do so.

NO-CALL FALL HUNTING SECRETS

How To Find Good Gobbler Country

During a no-call hunt, the quickest way to find an area occupied by fall gobblers is to go all out to find big fresh tracks. As previously indicated, fall gobblers will rarely be traveling with flocks of hens and poults, and will usually be alone or in groups of a few birds. Young turkeys, however, will usually be banded together, often in large flocks with their mother hens.

Moving along back roads or trails is the quickest way to find fall gobbler tracks in most areas. If there's snow on the ground, the big fresh tracks of gobblers will stand out like a sore thumb. If there's no snow, it pays to disregard hard, rocky and leaf-covered areas, and to concentrate the search

A good stand at a watering area often pays off especially in arid western mountains.

in sandy or muddy areas. If you cross big gobbler tracks which are *old,* start cutting wide circles through the area and look for fresh ones. If you cross hen and poult tracks (imprints of both large and small birds) and you want a gobbler, start circling and looking for gobbler tracks. The chances are a gobbler or two won't be far away. In the arid West, also check for tom tracks around every isolated waterhole.

Combining Stalking And Stand-Hunting Tactics

The surest way to nail a gobbler on a fall no-call hunt is through a combination of stalking and stand hunting. The hunt should begin in an area where fresh tom tracks are located. Then a careful stalk through the woods should be executed. The stalk should have two objectives: to enable you to see and kill a gobbler, and this failing, to locate promising spots for stand hunts later on.

Early- and late-hour stalks should be concentrated in a general area where you judge gobblers are likely to roost. Remember, in mountain or hill country, roosts are almost always found in tall pines or hardwoods on *southern* slopes. And in flat country, they are usually found in trees standing in swamps or stream bottoms. Also remember that turkey roosts will rarely be found more than a quarter-mile from water. Again, as previously indicated, roosts in regular use are sometimes easy to identify by fresh droppings under roost trees, by scarred tree branches, and sometimes by feathers under the trees.

Of course, the hunter should remember that turkeys do not *always* roost in the same area. Eastern turkeys occasionally roost wherever night overtakes them. Western turkeys are far more inclined to use exactly the same roosts. But any turkey flock may use a given roost only every *second* or *third* night. So, you may have to hunt any roost area several days to score.

Stalking can also pay off when conducted in areas where old toms are likely to feed and noon. In the fall, gobblers in most sections of the country feed heavily on acorns, so working areas with a concentration of oak brush or trees is often a

Merriam turkey roosts in particular can often be located by watching for feathers and droppings under big trees.

productive midmorning or midafternoon tactic. Gobblers like to noon in dry shadowy areas especially under large pines or hardwoods on hill or mountain slopes, or on dry mounds or hammocks in flat country, so stalking is usually most productive in this type terrain during the midday hours.

Stalking a fall gobbler is difficult, but no more so than stalking a wary whitetail buck. The key secret to successful stalking is to ease along very slowly, pausing every few yards to look and listen. Old gobblers will sometimes cluck or yelp, and even gobble quietly in the fall, especially when they have been split up and are attempting to re-group.

To get within gun or bow range of fall toms, the stalker should also take every possible advantage of terrain and cover. He should skirt the edges of clearings and stay in the timber. He should hunt perpendicular to ridges. In the more open West, binoculars are a great aid in spotting toms from ridge-tops or across thinly wooded country, and in areas where rifles are legal and used, this is all it takes. But most hunters prefer the challenge of closing to shotgun or bow range. And many gobblers sighted on a stalk hunt, especially in the East,

No-call stalking can pay off in spring or fall. Main tricks are to locate good gobbler country, to hunt perpendicular to ridges, and to move along very slowly and to stop for long periods to look and listen.

are jumped at close range and usually in brush, and only a fast swinging shotgun plus a dose of luck can give you a reasonable kill probability.

Fall Stand-Hunting Tactics That Pay Off

Sharp stand hunting near a roost also is a deadly tactic for nailing a fall gobbler without a call. The toms usually roost so late and leave the roost so early that they cannot be legally shot off the roost in most states. The hunter should choose a stand that will put him where the bird will likely be during the *first legal* shooting minutes during the morning and during the *last legal* shooting minutes during the afternoon. In mountain or hill country, this usually is an easy stand location to judge . . . for gobblers will usually fly from the roost to the first downhill clearing.

In flat country, it is sometimes possible to judge the area a gobbler will fly to when leaving a roost by checking sign in the roost area. Concentrated big tracks, and scratchings with big tracks in them and fairly close to a roost, usually indicate the gobbler will fly in that direction. In such a situation, the best stand location usually is about 150 yards from the roost in the direction of the gobbler sign. This is because flat-country gobblers, if undisturbed, will usually glide down close to the roost tree, then preen their feathers and loaf for ten or fifteen minutes before ambling on to feed. It's usually legal shooting time by the time they get 150 yards or so from the roost.

Of course, an old gobbler may pass wide of you and out of range. When he does so, the best no-call tactic is to let him get out of sight, then to make a wide circle with the objective of getting about 200 yards ahead of him. A stand at this point can give you another chance to waylay him.

NO-CALL SPRING HUNTING SECRETS

How To Pinpoint Good Hunting Areas

The best method for pinpointing good spring gobbler country for a no-call hunt is to combine a search for tracks with listening for gobbles. In the spring, gobblers, of course, tend to travel with hens, so locating any fresh turkey tracks is a sure sign gobblers are in the area. And, of course, their booming gobbles can be heard for long distances.

When reconnoitering for spring gobbler hangouts, it pays to spend each first hour or two of daylight listening for gobbles, and all day looking for tracks. Mark well each area where tracks are found, whether they are fresh or old. Then, listen for gobbles from these points at first light on succeeding mornings. Start by listening from points where tracks are freshest. The chances are high that you'll hear a spine-tingling gobble from one such listening point, especially if the morning is still and clear. If not, tracks alone are still a good departure point for a successful no-call hunt.

A Pattern For Spring Gobbler Stalking

Let's assume that you've arrived at a point where you located turkey tracks the preceding day. It's thirty minutes before the first crack of daylight, the latest any no-call gobbler hunt should begin. You're straining your ears. You hear the "whoo-whoo-whoo-whut-whoo" of an owl off in the blackness. Almost immediately the owl is answered by a faraway gobble. You turn on your flashlight and check the direction of the gobble with your compass, then head into the black woods. You can move without wasting time because you were wise enough to equip yourself with good waterproof boots, and with wool trousers and shirt or long johns under your camouflage suit to ward off briars and thorns.

You move as fast as you can straight toward the point of the gobble. In spots, going is slow and tough because of thick brush, a swamp, and areas of fallen timber. As the sky begins to gray in the east, you stop and listen intently, for you know you may be nearing the gobbler's position. You hear nothing, so you imitate the barred owl's hoot. You are rocked to the soles of your boots by an earth-shattering gobble which you judge is still almost a quarter-mile ahead.

You've *got* to get closer before your trophy leaves the roost. This time you set your course by the gray in the eastern sky and move with all possible speed. You hear another gobble as you crash through the woods, but you don't slow down yet. At last, you feel you are near the roost and you stop and listen. Now, a gobble roars out 200 yards ahead but a little to your left. Is it another tom? Or has your quarry flown from his roost?

Again, a gobble rings out a few degrees to your left—but none sounds from straight ahead. This time the gobble is muffled. You know the old tom has left the roost and will probably amble slowly in the same direction he flew. The sun is almost up. You now begin a quiet sneak to a projected point ahead of the gobbler. There you wait. Then another booming gobble rings out very near. You search the brush ahead just as it is touched by the first rays of the new sun. Suddenly you see black movement—and the most beautiful trophy in the world materializes within point-blank range! The long black beard drops almost to the ground. The warty head and beady radar eyes are turned away from you. You raise your gun or bow—and one of hunting's greatest moments is yours forever.

Of course, few no-call spring gobbler hunts will be this easy, but many will begin with that same long dash in the dark toward a thundering gobble. And some will pay off just as this one did. More often, however, your first frenzied attempt to intercept a roosting gobbler will fail. But even then, the attempt is worth the effort, for it narrows down the search area for the next morning's hunt. It may even enable you to find the old tom's roost. If so, the same roost-stand tactics already discussed for fall hunting also can pay big dividends late that same spring afternoon or early the next morning. And stalking through promising feeding areas or nooning areas can also pay off in the spring as well as in the fall—even if you never hear a gobble or find a roost.

Other Pay-Off No-Call Tactics

When easing along with the objective of spotting and stalking a spring gobbler, several precautions are all-important. As in fall hunting, you should sneak along slowly and quietly and pause for long periods to look and listen—for the fundamental requirement in this kind of no-call hunting is to spot an old tom before he spots you. Long pauses increase your chances of seeing or hearing turkeys, and decrease the turkey's chances of seeing or hearing you. In open country, this kind of stalking strategy, enhanced by the use of binoculars, provides a high probability of seeing turkeys a long distance away. Even in heavily timbered country, this kind of strategy provides you with a good probability of spotting turkeys at close range before you are spotted. Careful listening during these long pauses also pays off even if you don't hear a gobble. For, as already stressed, soft clucks or yelps of hens or gobblers may be your first clues to a spring gobbler's location.

As in fall hunting, it's also important to move through good cover whenever possible and never to step unnecessarily into open clearings. And whenever possible, the spring stalker should also work along perpendicular to ridges, ease to the top of each carefully and study the terrain beyond thoroughly before exposing himself.

There will be occasions, of course, when your first contact with a spring gobbler will be at point-blank range. More often, however, a properly executed stalk will result in spotting an old gobbler or flock of turkeys a considerable distance ahead. In this situation, the calm and crafty hunter usually has an excellent chance to study terrain and cover in relation to the position and movement of his quarry, and then to sneak or crawl within sure shotgun or bow range.

What To Do When You Look Down A Gobbler's Throat

When the new turkey stalker suddenly finds himself looking down the throat of a gobbler, the big bird will always look much closer than it really is. This is the time to be cool and collected. The hunter should force himself to remain still and to study the situation. If he does this, his quarry will often amble closer or walk behind a bush or embankment which the hunter can use as cover for a stalk to point-blank range. If the hunter has done his pre-hunt planning well, he'll also hear that stern voice inside cautioning "Don't fire unless you see a good beard." And when he identifies his gobbler, the hunter will still delay his shot until he is certain that his target is far enough away from other turkeys to insure he won't kill or cripple another when he shoots.

When a gobbler spots a hunter at close range, the old bird may either flush or run. The hunter, of course, should have no compunction about taking the gobbler either way. A crafty gobbler is always difficult enough a target, especially for the no-call hunter, and very fair game in the air or on the ground.

The following quick-look checklist of typical no-call turkey hunting situations and best tactics for each may also serve as a useful guide for new hunters. (See opposite page.)

NO-CALL HUNTING IN THE SNOW

Tracks in a fresh snow present the easiest of all turkey hunting situations for the man without a call. Tracks on snow which fell the night before the hunt or earlier the same day are bound to be so fresh that the turkeys will not be far ahead. Fresh tracks in an old snow usually are equally easy to identify and follow. In these ideal situations, the trick is to follow the tracks very quietly and slowly, taking advantage of all available cover, and to watch for black movement in the woods ahead. After leaving their roost near sunup, turkeys feed along slowly in frigid weather, spend most of the midday hours in one spot, then feed slowly back to their roost in the late afternoon. Therefore, the hunter does not have to hurry to overtake them. And when there's snow on the ground, turkeys are easily seen for considerable distances.

Of course, it is possible that the turkeys may see the hunter first. If this occurs, the hunter will know it; for the tracks at that point will become widely spaced, indicating the birds are running. If this occurs, the hunter often has no real problem if he will wait for twenty or thirty minutes before resuming his stalk. Most likely the birds, after running for a short distance and if not pressed, will calm down and forget the past danger. By patiently bird-dogging the turkeys ahead, the hunter is almost certain to sight the birds finally at some

NO-CALL TURKEY HUNTING CHECKLIST

Situation	Best Time to Hunt	Best Way to Hunt
1. Location of roost-fly-down clearing —or feeding route from roost area known.	From first light until 30 minutes after sunup; from 4 p.m. till end of legal shooting hours.	From stand overlooking clearing or point on feeding route some 150 yards from roost.
2. General roost area known.	From first light until 30 minutes after sunup.	Listen for tom flying down or gobbling. Then stalk him.
3. Location of strutting or watering area known.	From one hour after sunup until about 10 a.m.	From stand overlooking area.
4. Location of well defined nooning area known.	From about 11 a.m. until 2 p.m.	From stand overlooking area.
5. Location of nooning areas scattered over wide area known.	From about 11 a.m. until 2 p.m.	Ease slowly through area watching for gobbler. When gobbler spotted, stalk him.
6. Location of well-defined feeding area known.	From sunup till about 10 a.m.; from 3 p.m. until sundown.	From stand overlooking area.
7. Location of feeding areas scattered over wide area known.	From sunup till about 10 a.m.; from 3 p.m. until sundown.	Ease slowly through area watching for gobbler. When gobbler spotted, stalk him.

Slowly bird-dogging the tracks of a gobbler in the snow is the surest way to take turkeys without a call.

point where cover and terrain will permit a stalk within shooting range. At worst, he will run out of daylight in the general area where the turkeys are roosting—and he can resume his hunt from there early the next morning. A few states do not permit hunting turkeys in the snow, so be sure this tactic is legal in your area before using it.

Other no-call snow hunting tactics will be detailed in the following chapter.

CHAPTER 14

A No-Call Duel With A Wyoming Gobbler

Only my head protruded above my hiding place in the thick carpet of glistening fall snow. The twigs of a fallen pine branch added to my concealment and I hoped to the accomplishment of my objective. By now my body was so numb I hardly felt the bitter cold. I squinted my watering eyes and through the bare twigs I studied the white pine-, oak-, and aspen-fringed clearing before me. Even with unfeeling hands, I managed to make another gobbler cluck with my old box. Again an answering "cluck-cluck-cluck" rang out from across the clearing!

The old Merriam slowly materialized, a majestic black statue surveying the white wilderness. Then the great bird bulldozed his way through the snow to the center of the clearing. His long neck was erect. His warty head jerked from side to side. His penetrating eyes continued to sweep every inch of the surrounding countryside. His long beard almost touched the snow.

I tried not to move, yet my body trembled in its cold

burrow and my thumb quivered in its search for the gun safety. At that moment, the sun punched its way through a swirling snow cloud and turned the black gobbler into a bird of paradise. Almost every color of the rainbow now radiated from the old monarch's shining body. His warty head was now a vivid blue with white crown. His rump had turned to creamy white and his tail to soft chestnut tipped with pure white. If this majestic bird would walk but a few steps closer, I would at last have my supreme trophy—and those long days of fighting the blizzard-swept wilderness would be amply rewarded.

The sudden burst of sunlight not only radiated from the shiny feathers of my quarry. It also danced on that six inches of my gun barrel protruding above the snow. The gobbler's sharp eyes zeroed in on this tell-tale reflection. My dreams

If you're after beautiful Merriam turkeys, there's no better place to hunt than Wyoming or Colorado.

were shattered as he burst into the air and glided back into the dense pines and aspens. Slowly, I rose and forced my numb body back toward the Bronco which was half buried in a snow-filled gully two long miles to the east.

Very late that night, I thawed out in a warm bed at the Apache Motel in Sundance, Wyoming. I reflected upon my four days of fall gobbler gunning in the surrounding Black Hills, a rugged and beautifully forested country with plenty of elusive Merriam turkeys and some of the biggest-racked mule deer and whitetailed bucks I have ever encountered.

My failure to take that giant Black Hills gobbler was due to my failure to observe one simple yet basic precaution. I had not wound black or camouflage tape around my gun barrel to keep the sun from reflecting from it. I cussed my stupid carelessness and promised to rectify this oversight before the morning hunt.

The three days leading up to this exciting encounter with that wise old Black Hills gobbler had been hard but satisfying ones. With the aid of my four-wheel-drive vehicle, chains, and shovel, I had navigated many miles of snow-covered, blizzard-swept wilderness trying to pinpoint big tracks signaling an area occupied by a trophy gobbler—that first and most important task on a western gobbler hunt. During this long reconnaissance for trophy gobbler sign, I could have killed hens and poults easily. Although hens and poults are legal game in most fall hunting areas in the Rocky Mountain states, I was after a trophy tom. For this reason I had passed up all hen and poult sign and had concentrated my search for the tracks of big gobblers in distant areas, knowing old long-bearded western monarchs prefer to batch it during the fall months in rugged areas remote from those occupied by flocks of hens and poults.

Those long days of searching for gobbler sign in ever deepening snow had been satisfying for another reason. This search had taught me just how fast Merriam gobblers in mountain country will move to low country when the big snows set in. When the hunt started, I had reliable information less than a week old, on gobbler sightings in the Black Hills' high country, but these sightings had occurred just before the heavy

November snows. Three long days of searching these high country areas had failed to result in the sighting of one fresh gobbler track. I began searching the low country on the morning of the fourth day, and almost immediately I had picked up the tracks of a trophy gobbler, the same old bird I had called up—then let get away the eventful afternoon just past.

As I wound dull tire tape around the barrel of my twelve, I pondered my strategy for the following morning. Would I try to call up the old gobbler again, or would I attempt to stalk him? I attempted to analyze similar situations in past hunts and the results of employing each of these two basic gobbler hunting strategies. I reviewed the times I had hunted for Merriam gobblers in Colorado's prime turkey country near Aguilar, Trinidad, Pagosa Springs, and on the wild Uncompahgre Plateau, so similar to this Wyoming Black Hills country, in Utah's Manti-Lasal National Forest, and in New Mexico's prime turkey country near Raton, Reserve, Pinon, Magdalena, and Silver City. One key consideration emerged from my motel room play-back of these exciting hunts: I had never been able to call up a fully mature Merriam gobbler in the fall on the day after I had spooked him! Since the old tom had been spooked, and I had the chance to bird-dog him in deep snow, I decided on a no-call stalk hunt. Then I slept.

The snow and the wind had stopped. Through the sub-zero pre-dawn air, lighted by a yellow moon, I could see the snowy silhouette of a mountain peak ten miles away. Pinks and yellows signaling the birth of day burst slowly across the eastern sky. Sipping hot coffee from my thermos, and warm enough in my two pairs of thermal underwear, insulated rubber boots, heavy wool trousers and jacket, I sat upon a comfortable stump waiting for a clear view of the countryside below. I had to conclude that two of the biggest rewards which come from years of gobbler hunting are chances like this to survey wild and remote country which few others ever see and the almost mystic ability the old turkey hunter develops to sweep his eyes across gobbler country and to predict where and when his elusive quarry will move across it.

Before sunlight touched the clearing where the old tom had outwitted me the afternoon before, my eyes had determined where he was now roosting, the exact clearing he would fly down into in the next twenty minutes, and the thick, head-high clumps of scrub oaks he would spend the morning in scratching for acorns.

There was only one hollow with big pines and a southern exposure on the ridge lying north of the valley I overlooked. I *knew* the old gobbler had roosted here at dusk in order to enjoy both the safety of a high roost and protection from the north wind. A two or three acre clearing punctured the thick hillside forest a few hundred yards below this hollow. Since this was the only close clearing downhill from the old gobbler's roost, I knew he would fly from the roost directly into it.

Finally, my eyes told me that the only plentiful supply of acorns in the area lay under a scattered clump of big oaks in the valley immediately below the clearing. I knew the gobbler would amble down from the clearing to feed there, probably by an hour after sunup. I knew I would not have time to reach the clearing before the old tom flew into it. So, I finished my coffee, headed for the feeding area, and selected a stand overlooking the line of oaks. There was a possibility of the old gobbler walking within shotgun range of my stand as he moved down from the fly-down clearing to feed. Even if he entered the feeding area by another route, I knew I would be able to pick up his tracks by midmorning and begin my stalk.

The stand was a good one. A pine stump constituted a comfortable seat, one which I could easily sit still on for long periods. The screen of bare aspen and oak branches about me afforded adequate concealment, yet the branches were thin enough to permit me to see through them in all directions. Yes, if I remained still and could forego a cigarette for the next hour, my chances of taking the big gobbler without moving from this stand were good—provided the old bird took the shortest route to the line of oak clumps I knew he would feed in.

I opened the action of my old full-choke twelve to make certain I had loaded the right shells in the earlier darkness. Yes, the long three-inch magnum shells were loaded in the proper order: a 1⅞ ounce charge of #4's, followed by two heavy loads of BB's.

The bright sun climbed slowly in the cloudless sky and the white winter wonderland about me sparkled like a sea of diamonds. I waited and watched the whiteness for black movement. I felt a sudden and deep thanksgiving that the stately Merriam, in my opinion the most majestic of America's wild turkeys, was still abundant across large areas of the West, and that this great bird would still be thriving to thrill generations of hunters yet unborn.

Suddenly, my eyes caught black movement far ahead in the whiteness! The big gobbler was entering the line of oak clumps 300 yards to my right, but he was moving *away* from my position. It was time to start a stalk. I edged down into the valley floor behind the nearest clump of oaks. Slowly, I made my way toward the point where the old tom had entered the oak-fringed valley. I knew the gobbler would probably continue to feed slowly through the oaks directly away from my line of approach. However, there was a chance that he would reverse directions and begin feeding toward me. Therefore, I approached each clump of oaks stealthily, peered around it, and scanned the whiteness ahead carefully before making my way to the next oak clump. The fresh fallen snow was soft, without crust, and my steps generated no noise.

I was almost an hour in reaching the point where my quarry entered the oak-lined valley. I looked down upon the largest gobbler tracks I had ever seen. This bird was bound to weigh twenty pounds! Goose pimples ran up and down my spine. The real test now lay immediately ahead. I had to execute a stalk which would close me to within 40 yards of this cagy, radar-eyed old bird, for I would not chance crippling him with a longer shot.

Slowly I forged ahead in the general direction of the big tracks, but using each succeeding clump of oaks to study the valley floor ahead and to shield my creeping approach. As I suspected, the old gobbler was feeding slowly from one oak clump to the next. This was evidenced by close-spaced tracks and great ovals in the snow scratched out down to brown leaves and earth below. I knew I would overtake my quarry shortly and that the outcome of the duel would rest upon which of us spotted the other first. I proceeded, straining my eyes against the glistening whiteness to win this critical duel.

The encounter was so unexpected, it was over before I could realize that it had happened! I had just eased up to a thick oak clump, head high and about 20 yards in diameter. As I started to peer around the left side of the clump, I sensed, almost uncannily, a presence to my right. I turned my head and found myself staring into beady eyes peering at me from the opposite side of the oak clump. I could only see a warty head and those beady eyes. Then the head and eyes were gone, but I continued to stare at where they had been almost in disbelief.

By the time I recovered my senses, the gobbler was emerging from the line of oaks 100 yards away and was running head down and as fast as a greyhound straight up a steep bare ridge to my left. In this situation, most old turkey chasers would have waited an hour for the bird to settle down, then resumed bird-dogging his tracks. I would have done so, except that this situation was almost identical to another I had experienced in Colorado years before. The top and opposite side of the bare ridge the old gobbler was running up was heavily timbered, the same situation which had prevailed on the Colorado hunt. Then, I had simply walked to the opposite side of the ridge, taken a stand in the timber and that old Aguilar gobbler had walked right down to me looking back over his shoulder. So I executed the same tactic in my final attempt to intercept the big Black Hills gobbler.

My route to the opposite side of the ridge the gobbler was still running up was shorter and less steep than that the gobbler would have to take if he continued to the top of the ridge, then moved down the opposite side. Ten minutes later, I reached a comfortable stump overlooking a wide area of scattered pines directly downhill from the point where I judged the old gobbler had topped the ridge. Motionless and facing uphill, I waited. I wondered if there was really a chance that this unusual tactic would again pay off a second time.

Suddenly, a huge black form was actually descending toward me. Down the steep white wall of the ridge it moved, a few yards at a time. Through the brown and white ponderosa trunks it came. It held close to the pine trunks for cover. My thumb shook, but I managed to ease off the safety. Slowly, the black form turned into my majestic Black Hills gobbler. Now, each time it paused, I could see its warty head and sharp eyes searching the uphill slopes to see if I was following. Straight down to me, my supreme trophy came, growing larger with every step. He looked like a great and beautiful mirage. Without question, this was the largest Merriam I had ever had in gun range.

My old Black Hills gobbler fell in the snow, but only after one of the toughest hunts I've ever enjoyed.

Now my supreme trophy was a scant 30 yards away, still searching the uphill slopes, still completely unaware of my presence. The cardinal rule of all sensible gobbler gunners was imprinted on my brain: "Take your gobbler the moment of first sure opportunity—for that moment may come only once!" But somehow this moment was too special to be shackled by any rule, even this one. The gobbler stood only ten feet from the safety of a thick oak clump should he decide to run—and his chances of eluding my gun, should he choose to flush through the screen of big pines, would be even higher. I simply could not take the magnificent bird where he stood. This greatest duel of my life, whether successful or not, had to end on a higher plane.

I stood up. The gobbler gambled on the short dash to the safety of the oaks. For a moment I thought his dash was faster than the swing of my gun. My shot echoed and died in the Black Hills stillness. For a long second, there was no other sound. I prepared to make my way back to the Bronco, once more empty-handed and defeated. Then, suddenly, I heard the mighty flapping of wings! And a whirlwind of black feathers and snow funneled into the clear air above the oak brush. Two pellets had made their way into a warty head. This old monarch didn't quite weigh twenty pounds, but he had a handsome ten-inch beard. I had finally won the grueling Black Hills duel after all.

Hunters who would like to duplicate this exciting hunt in the best Merriam turkey country in the West should write the Wyoming Game and Fish Commission for permit applications at the address listed in Appendix I.

CHAPTER 15

The Colorado Gobbler
That Wouldn't Die

Like a ghost rising from the ground, the big gobbler materialized just out of gun range. For a fleeting moment, the huge silhouette zig-zagged through the pine shadows ahead—then disappeared racing uphill and to my left. I stood stone-still until I knew the gobbler was well up the steep mountain face. Then I turned left and moved quickly to the next ridge. I climbed the ridge to a point where it was intersected by a high rim rock cliff slanting down from the lofty area the old tom was headed for.

I sat down on a pine stump facing the uphill base of the cliff and waited. I knew the gobbler would either fly to the top of the cliff when he reached it, or more likely, slink back down along its edge to this area. I had an excellent chance of intercepting one of the biggest and most audacious Merriam gobblers I had ever hunted—a reward which had stemmed primarily from my intimate familiarity with this prime turkey range and its long-bearded rulers.

I was well hidden in a clump of thick oak brush. Ten

yards ahead, a narrow grassy clearing began and cut through the brush for 100 yards uphill along the base of the sheer cliff. The white-frosted floor of the clearing was spotlighted by the intense rays of the midmorning Colorado sun. If the old Merriam came, I would first see him on this bright and shining stage!

And the gobbler came, tiptoeing slowly, peering back over his shoulder to see if danger was following. The giant bird froze on the far edge of the clearing—an awe-inspiring statue of soft chestnut, creamy rump, and a *right wing which was almost pure white!*

His long neck and red warty head now formed a prying periscope which scanned above the waist-high oak brush, first along the back trail, then to the right, then to the left, then straight ahead where I was hiding. I could feel those sharp eyes burning through the wall of oak brush and straight into my greedy, pounding heart. How the old gobbler made me out, I'll never know. But he did. Suddenly, his head went down —his blurred mass streaked into the thick brush—and the frosted clearing was empty.

I rose slowly from the stump. On the horizon to my right, the 12,000-foot Spanish Peaks, or "Twin Sisters," steep, smug, and snow-capped, seemed once more amused by the spectacle of my easy defeat by old White Wing, one of the largest and craftiest gobblers they had ever mothered.

"So, you're still chasing that old white winged freak—you must be nuts! That old bird's got a charmed life and he's smarter than all the hunters in the Spanish Peaks put together!" In spite of the insult, I handed Hugh Jones a cup of coffee. "I've got this afternoon and tomorrow left, and I don't intend to close the season without another *real* try for that old sultan."

Hugh gulped down his coffee, grinned knowingly again and headed out on patrol. As the brusque State Wildlife Conservation Officer disappeared in his white sedan, I felt a special debt of gratitude to him. Hugh and his deputy, Cliff Moser, had been instrumental in the purchase by the Colorado Division of Wildlife of the more than 1500 acres of prime Merriam turkey range I was now hunting on. And through the efforts of these hard working officers, landowners in the area had opened another parcel of adjoining land of comparable size to public hunting. It was good knowing that this vast "Spanish Peaks Wildlife Management Area," 18 miles west of Aguilar, would provide superb gobbler hunting for the public for years to come.

Old White Wing was indeed a freak of nature, the only tom I had ever seen with a white wing, and the craftiest Merriam I have ever dueled. I knew he would probably roost

Colorado's Spanish Peaks area offers some of the West's best hunting for big Merriam turkeys.

that night in one of two pine-studded hollows just under the rimrock high above camp. I had spent days locating these roosts, and I knew they were the only ones being used regularly in the area. At each roost, the high limbs of big pines were shorn of bark. Green pine branches, feathers and piles of both fresh and old droppings coated the carpet of dry pine needles below. The soft ground around the roosts was pitted with tracks of all sizes, indicating that both roosts were being used by hens and poults as well as gobblers, a very unusual occurrence in the fall when old gobblers usally roost alone.

As the afternoon sun dropped low, I was on station overlooking a large clearing 200 yards below the northernmost roost, the one nearest to the last spot where I had seen the old white winged gobbler that morning. In the shadowy hours, a large flock of hens and poults, then three young gobblers crossed the clearing. Just as legal shooting time ended, I saw the dim forms of two gobblers slink past—and one was large enough to be old White Wing. Then, in the darkening air I heard the thunder of turkeys flying to bed. I turned on my flashlight and worked my way back to camp.

In the warm goose down bed of my one-man trailer, I sipped on a last cup of after-dinner coffee. I gazed into the soft light of my Coleman lantern and visioned my past encounters with old White Wing, and each was still wildly exciting! My first encounter with this sly old ghost bird had taken place in a dazzling world of contrasts: patches of brilliant midday clashing with patches of black shadows in a world of giant ponderosa pines on a high ridgetop. This was three years ago, before John Sakarisen retired and sold this wild and fertile turkey county to the state so that "his" turkeys would continue to be managed properly. I was hunting the high ponderosa country for it is here where old Merriams like to noon. The big gobbler stepped out of a patch of shadows into a sunlit clearing. I, too, had just moved into open sunlight. The crafty old bird knew he was out of range. For a long second we stared at each other and etched on my memory forever was the sight of a gobbler too big to be a gobbler, a gobbler with a beard too long and massive to be a beard, and with a right wing which was almost pure white! That was my last glimpse of old White Wing that season, and the last day I settled for a young tom with a four-inch beard.

The following fall I hunted ten days, but not once did I sight old White Wing. On the last day I took an old 18-pound tom with a respectable nine-inch beard, but I went home remorseful, thinking my gobbler of gobblers had not survived the rugged winter.

On my third day of hunting this season, I roosted six big toms and discovered that old White Wing was still around. At first light that next morning I was hidden at the edge of the first big clearing downhill from the roost. One at a time, the big birds thundered off the roost and sat down in the clearing not 20 yards from the end of my gun barrel. *And the last bird to hit the clearing was old White Wing!* He clucked, flapped his wings, and fluffed his feathers. Half again as big as the other toms, he stomped the frosted grass, then tiptoed straight toward me until he was not 10 yards away— but it was still five minutes before legal shooting time!

In that sub-zero weather, sweat poured off my face. My legs began shaking in uncontrollable jerks. For an eternity it seemed as though the hand on my watch had frozen. Then with one minute to go before legal shooting time, *and for no earthly reason,* old White Wing burst into the air and sailed out of sight over the pine tops. The other gobblers didn't fly. They just stood still in the clearing begging for me to shoot. I wanted only that old gobbler with a white right wing. I walked into the clearing and the five stupid gobblers ducked into the oak brush.

But tomorrow would be another day. I finished my coffee, lit a last cigarette and replayed my encounter with old White Wing in the sunlit clearing that morning. And the more I thought about it, the surer I was that old White Wing was one of the gobblers I saw go to roost that evening. Finally, I turned off the lantern and snuggled down for good into my warm feather bed. Tomorrow *had* to be the day!

Thirty minutes before dawn, I was settled on a log overlooking the same clearing I had seen the turkeys pass through to roost the evening before. The clearing was straight downhill from the roost, so I knew the odds were good that the turkeys would fly down into it. How I hoped old White Wing would be among them.

Suddenly, brush crashed below. Then a few minutes later, four other hunters stumbled past me straight uphill toward the roost. I knew these noisy hunters would spook every turkey off the roost far ahead of shooting time and that any old gobblers there would soon flush far down the ridge, instead of pitching into the clearing.

As fast as I could pick my way along in the blackness, I moved perpendicular to the ridgetop and gradually uphill. At the first crack of dawn, I had reached the top of the ridge about a quarter-mile west of the roost. The oak brush and pines were far thicker along this section of the ridge than to the east. I had gambled the only way I could: that when the gobblers were spooked off their roost they would head in this direction.

As the eastern sky turned full pink I was panting hard, but I was perched on a high boulder where I could survey the country about me in all directions. Suddenly, I heard the swishing, drumming wings of flying turkeys. One big gobbler glided below me and lit in a stand of tall pines nearly a half mile beyond and well down the side of the ridge. A few seconds later, another gobbler flew right over my head. The massive wings froze into a glide just after the gobbler passed by and the right wing was much lighter than the other! I watched intently as the glide continued. The big bird finally fluttered down on the ridgetop several hundred yards above the pines where the first gobbler had lit.

Legal shooting time was now only a few minutes away. The waist-high oak brush was far too thick for a successful stalk. Watching these two gobblers going to roost together the night before and now seeing them fly off the roost in the same general direction suddenly took on high significance. This fall, old White Wing had a permanent buddy. He was batching it with another old gobbler! These two spooked gobblers would probably try to get back together again a couple of hours after the woods quieted down. My most promising strategy was now obvious.

I headed swiftly down the side of the ridge to a point about midway between where the two gobblers had lit. I sat down on a pine stump overlooking an old logging trail winding through the thick oak brush. This trail would be the obvious route for both gobblers to take when they began their rendezvous. Oak brush was growing back in the trail, but it was spotted and only a couple of feet high. I could see reasonably well for about 40 yards both up and down the trail. Just as I got settled, I knew the wait would be a long one. A barrage of shotgun blasts boomed from the general area of the roost and I knew the four hunters who had spooked the gobblers had gotten into the hens and poults, which were also legal game.

I waited patiently for quietness to return to the woods, as I knew the old gobblers would also do before calling to each other and beginning their rendezvous. What a world old White Wing lived in! This rugged expanse of golden oaks, scattered pines, grassy clearings, tiny mirror springs, boulders and rimrock was his fall and winter world, a world which nurtured and protected him from hunger and hunters and the great snows. And to the west old White Wing's lofty spring and summer world, the Twin Sisters, loomed high on the blue horizon. Here, under a scraggly fir or in a thick white-barked aspen clump, old White Wing probably hatched out a half dozen years ago. And to this high world he had surely migrated each spring to collect his own harem and to sire his own young. Lord, what a bird this old white-winged gobbler was!

Suddenly, I realized that the barrage of shots from the roost area had long subsided. Even the occasional spasmodic shots which followed had ceased. Stillness now dominated the woods. The stillness, absolute except for faint rustlings of oak leaves and the distant cries of a lonesome sapsucker, held for another hour—then two.

A short, cautious "Where-are-you?" *gobble* rang from the top of the ridge! Two minutes later, old White Wing was answered with an identical gobble from the clump of pines below. Neither gobbler had moved ten yards from where it had landed at dawn. But now, they would be coming together and I could not have been in a more likely spot to observe their rendezvous. Ten minutes later the two gobblers checked with each other again, this time with loud clucks. These told me that both birds were moving straight for my area, probably along the overgrown logging trail. That old, familiar sweat was beginning to run down my face and those uncontrollable body shakes were beginning to set in. I checked the safety on my gun and gave myself a stern order to remain calm.

The third exchange of position reports between the two sly old birds was a series of soft clucks very close to my position. I judged old White Wing to be less than 100 yards straight uphill and the other gobbler to be less than half that distance straight downhill. Moving nothing but my eyes, I studied the uphill stretch of the logging trail intently. For ten long minutes I searched feverishly for a glimpse of that old White Wing gobbler, but I couldn't detect the slightest movement in the oak brush along the trail. Had that uncannny old devil sensed my presence and eluded me again?

A voice inside me yelled, "Stand up and look! Old White Wing is bound to be within range!" But I dared not gamble away my last chance to take this bird of my dreams. I was almost blinded by sweat now dropping through my eyelashes, but I remained stone still and searched with all my power with those wet eyes and with my ears.

Suddenly, I caught a flash of movement 40 yards uphill in the thick oaks on the far side of the trail. Then for a brief moment, my prized gobbler stood clearly in a small clearing with that white right wing shining like a patch of snow in the bright sun. Before I could raise my gun, the old gobbler disappeared behind a big ponderosa log. In a flash I did a thorough study of the situation. The cagy old gobblers were taking no chances. They were moving together in the thick oaks instead of along the open trail.

I wiped the sweat from my eyes. With my old twelve raised and ready, I stared at the oak brush. Suddenly, a big, warty head and long neck popped sykward above the log. My gun thundered, spewing out its lethal barrage of #4's. The oak brush exploded! A funnel of leaves, dust, and feathers spiralled upward and the roar of dying wings beating the

I didn't get old White Wing, but his buddy that I did bag was a magnificent gobbler I'll always be proud of.

brush and ground boomed in the still air. As the roar died and the funnel of leaves, dust, and feathers settled, I eased forward.

Just over the gray, decaying log, a dark and lifeless form was draped over a pile of broken oaks. I stopped and stared at the still black mass of feathers half hidden in the brush. The long duel was at last over—and where was the keen thrill of victory? In place of exuberance, a big lump was inching up my throat. Even a lousy coyote let go with a sad and eerie wail.

At that moment, I heard a rustle in the oak brush above. I turned and couldn't believe my eyes. *A gobbler too big to be a gobbler, with a beard too long to be a beard, and with a white right wing was staring at me from high above on the old logging trail!* "You sly old devil!" I yelled. And I laughed and laughed at that incomparable old ghost bird from the bottom of my belly. Old White Wing putted and lifted his massive body into the air with the ease of a spunky poult—and disappeared in a "V" of shimmering blueness between the snow-capped peaks of the Twin Sisters.

Old White Wing's buddy was quite a gobbler, certainly the best Merriam I ever bagged on a no-call hunt. He had a ten-inch beard and tipped the scales at nearly twenty pounds. I slung the big bird over my shoulder and, whistling like a kid, I headed home to wait once more for another chance at old White Wing. You might get him first if you write the Colorado Division of Wildlife (see Appendix I for address) for a permit to hunt the beautiful and productive Spanish Peaks Wildlife Area.

CHAPTER 16

Bowhunting Turkeys: The Ultimate Challenge

Dueling an edgy and sharp-eyed gobbler with a bow may be the toughest and most challenging form of big game hunting in America. It is precisely this monumental difficulty which gives gobbler hunting with a bow its unique mystique and charm: factors which entice thousands of archers into the field each spring and fall to try their hand at this sport of sports.

The goal of this chapter is to paint the thrills and pitfalls of bowhunting turkeys, and to increase the novice's chances of scoring in spite of the difficult odds. During bow seasons, when the woods are quiet and game is moving naturally, one can see more turkeys and learn more about them than at any other time. And in this kind of hunting, there's a stirring magic kinship with hunters from ages past. These factors alone make bowhunting turkeys worthwhile whether or not one is ever bagged. But hunting's always sweeter when there's a chance for success. This, too, can belong to the hunter willing to study the following text.

Chapter 1 covered those basic factors which should be considered in selecting and readying tackle for a turkey hunt with a bow. And all other chapters preceding this one detailed hunting tactics which are as applicable to bowhunting as to gun hunting. This chapter will proceed from there, first by walking the reader through each of the three hunts which gave the author a gobbler with a bow, then by discussing the finer points of bowhunting turkeys illustrated by these hunts.

Taking three wild gobblers with a bow may sound like an impossible feat, especially when it was accomplished in a four-year period. However, the author is quick to point out that he is lucky enough to spend more days studying and hunting turkeys each year than many hunters are able to do in a lifetime. For example, for many years, I have leap-frogged from state to state, hunting spring gobblers with either gun or bow—and almost every day from early March until late May. In addition, I usually hunt fall turkeys from early September into December or January. I should also point out that this chapter highlights only my three *successful* bow-hunts for gobblers as a basis for discussing hunting tactics. I have also struck *out* many, many times.

MY FIRST GOBBLER WITH A BOW

The November dawn was still an hour away—and crossing the swamp was rough. I sloshed through calf-deep mud and water. Thorny briars tore at my clothing and bow. But guided by flashlight and lured on by the promise ahead, I held my compass course through that soggy, snake-infested hell. My destination was a remote oak ridge where I had located the fresh and concentrated sign of feeding turkeys the day before. I made the top of the ridge just as daylight cracked and sat down on a stump to get my breath before scouting for a calling spot.

The woods grew brighter. I was in the very center of a wide-open area. Only a few scrub oaks and palmetto clumps protruded from the white sandy ground, but I could already make out a scattering of acorns—and turkey tracks—under the nearest oak. I had no chance to move to a shielded calling position. Without warning, the whirr of gliding wings filled the air and a big drove of turkeys started hitting the ground less than 100 yards away! In my completely exposed position, and without even an arrow strung, I could only remain frozen and hope for more favorable circumstances to develop.

Twenty minutes later, the birds had fed toward me and I was in the *center* of the whole flock! About twenty hens and big poults were scratching for acorns all around me, some so close I could almost reach out and touch them. The sun had now popped through the trees and the open ridge was lit up like a Christmas tree. Every few minutes, one of the old hens would stare intently at me from point-blank range, then sound off with a warning purr or an alarm putt. Every long periscope neck would go straight up and the birds would crouch ready for take-off. But I remained frozen and unidentified, thanks to my complete stillness and total camouflage of face, hands, clothing, and bow. Finally, the birds would begin feeding again.

For nearly an hour, I was a member of that turkey flock. I watched them go to full alert each time a crow called or a squirrel sounded off, then settle down to feeding again when they determined all was well. I was entranced by the antics of the lanky young gobblers with their minute stubby beards and reddish heads, and already taller than even the old hens. Like schoolboys, the young toms bunched together frolicking as they fed, always careful to ignore the females in the flock.

I could only watch the amazing panorama. With all those point-blank radar eyes on me, I had no chance to string an arrow, much less make a draw. Finally, the flock fed beyond me and to my left. Just as the last tom disappeared in the oaks at about 50 yards range, I decided to rush the flock, split them up, and gamble on calling one back later.

But at that second, I caught black movement and spotted an old gobbler far up the ridge in the direction from which the flock had sailed in. He disappeared behind a thick oak clump and I made my move. I ran to the clearing edge, knelt behind another oak clump and quickly strung an arrow. *If* the old tom hadn't spotted me, and *if* he followed the feeding path of the hens and poults, I might have a chance for a shot!

The old tom reappeared and moved slowly into range. He was a monstrous coal black monarch, and his long beard almost dragged the ground. I prayed for my hands to stop shaking and for the opportunity to make a draw.

There was one particularly high clump of palmettos in the center of the clearing and the tom was feeding straight toward it. I recomputed its range a dozen times in the next two minutes. It had to be exactly 18 yards away. My wildest dreams came true and the gobbler disappeared behind its green daggers. At that second, I made my draw still kneeling. The tom re-emerged on the other side of the clump, about 3 yards beyond it and facing sideways to me. I released with my 20-yard sight just above the exact center of his upper body.

The arrow struck home, black feathers flew, and my heart jumped in my throat. The gobbler exploded into the air—but dropped after flying less than 50 yards. The arrow

My first turkey with a bow was a beautiful Gulf Hammock gobbler. There's no better place to hunt in Florida. An Allen compound bow gave me all three of my bow-hit turkeys.

had gone straight through the upper body cavity. After many seasons of grueling work, painstaking planning, much suspense and many failures, I had finally taken my first gobbler with a bow—a fine 20-pounder with an eleven-inch beard. This unforgettable experience unfolded in 1970 in West Florida's Gulf Hammock Wildlife Management Area near the town of the same name.

MY SECOND GOBBLER WITH A BOW

I was lucky enough to take my second gobbler with a bow on an early spring morning in 1972. I was again hunting in Florida, this time near the Avon Park Bombing Range. My good fortune began the afternoon before when I was trying to roost two big gobblers in a swamp where I had located their fresh tracks. Just before dark, I heard the two birds gobble, then fly into the swamp from a tiny clearing about 100 yards from my position.

Well before daylight the next morning, I was in full camouflage and well hidden in an old fallen treetop on the clearing fringe. As I waited for the star-studded sky to silver, I scraped away all twigs and leaves from my blind floor and added a few branches to the treetop for better concealment. I found a spot where I could stand and ease my bow around to cover most of the open clearing. Then I leaned the bow, with an arrow nocked, in shooting position against the fallen tree trunk.

As dawn approached, my mind's eye could see those big black gobblers growing more and more restless on their cypress roost. At any moment, they could come plunging at me from their black swamp lair and fill the clearing with awesome radar-eyed nobility. I knew they would fly down into this same clearing from which they had propelled themselves up to their roost the evening before. And I would have to face them with that short-range bow, and somehow draw it—and release with cool precision. My goose pimples grew larger and larger and I almost wished that daylight would never come.

But suddenly dawn was upon me, and I steeled myself for the task ahead. With my old box cupped against my stomach, I stroked out two muffled clucks I knew the gobblers would hear. I eased the box back to the ground and picked up my bow. Song birds began chirping and an owl hooted far back in the swamp. Ten minutes passed, and the eastern sky turned pink. Then one of the old toms gobbled once for a verification of my position. But I knew he didn't need it. I drew my bow and checked my swing again across the clearing. Then resting the lower tip of the bow on a limb so that

When possible, the bowhunter should build a good blind, which he can just barely see and shoot over.

the sharp broadhead pointed at the center of the tiny clearing, I waited.

The sun was still hidden behind the swamp when I heard the first whirr of sailing wings. I froze with my bow ready for draw and watched the monstrous black glider come. The old swamp king hit the clearing 50 yards out in a position of full alert. For a full five minutes, his sharp eyes searched the clearing fringe for danger. Then, satisfied that all was well, he turned toward the swamp and gobbled. And a few seconds later, he was joined by the other tom.

Both birds began ruffing their feathers and stretching their giant wings. I seized this opportunity to ease my bow a few inches to the right so that it pointed straight in their direction. The gobblers then began moving toward me in half struts. As I waited for them to close to sure range, my bow felt as though it weighed 50 pounds, and I begged my heart to slow down and my hands not to shake.

Suddenly, one of the gobblers dropped his half-strut and began running to my right, chasing a grasshopper. My heart almost stopped. But the second old tom continued his leisurely stroll straight toward me. I was shielded so well in my blind that I gambled big. I waited until he was in scary, point-blank range. At that moment, facing directly toward me, he dropped his strut and looked back over his shoulder at the second gobbler—and I made my draw. I prayed for a smooth release and let the arrow fly with the 10-yard bead centered on the long neck at its juncture with the body.

Feathers flew and the gobbler began flopping wildly on the ground. The second tom exploded back into the swamp. At that moment I came completely unglued. My heart pounded like a bass drum and my whole body shook. I couldn't believe that magnificent 17-pound mass of black with a nine-inch beard, now lying still in the dew-tinted clearing, was really mine—that I had finally taken my second gobbler with a bow! The arrow had almost severed the neck from the body.

MY THIRD GOBBLER WITH A BOW

My third gobbler with a bow took my arrow while perched

high in a gnarled oak tree the following year, the fall of '73. And much of the credit for this triumph must go to Lady Luck and to my good friend Buck Ray of Ocala, Florida. Buck had invited me to hunt on his private ranch, primarily for deer. Although the Florida gun season was on, I had decided to go with the bow—and to hunt an area where Buck told me a particularly heavy-horned whitetail—and a flock of turkeys—was ranging.

I was easing down a muddy trail, one slow step at a time, when I glimpsed black movement in green palmettos some 100 yards ahead. I froze and a young gobbler materialized in the open trail feeding directly toward me! The late sun was just beginning to disappear in the thick wall of palms and oaks to my left.

Suddenly, a doe just off the trail winded me, snorted and bounced straight toward the turkey. The gobbler raced into the woods toward the pink western sky. I knew this commotion might well make the tom edgy enough to fly up to roost early, so I eased down the trail to the point where he had disappeared and waited in a clump of waist-high palmettos.

It would be legal to shoot until 6:00 p.m.—thirty minutes after sunset. I glanced at my watch. It was now 5:45. A few minutes later, the still air exploded with beating wings and a mass of black landed in a big oak tree some 50 yards away. Shielded by a thick clump of palm tops, I eased toward the turkey, but was stopped by a shoulder-high clump of palmettos.

I could see there was no way I could approach closer without spooking the gobbler. One rattle of the palmettos and he would be gone. I inched right a few feet and could now clearly see the gobbler just to the right of the palm tops. He was still in strong light in the top of the oak—and the forest floor where I crouched was growing dark, so I knew I could draw without being detected. But the range was long; 40 yards—no, nearer 45 yards. I glanced at my watch. Three minutes left! If I shot, it would have to be *now*. Facing straight away from me, the gobbler's vital head, neck, and upper back were in clear view, and all his lower body was shielded by a big oak limb. Thus, I would have little chance of crippling. I eased up the bow and held the 40-yard sight on his neck just above the body, then I released with all the calm I could muster.

The arrow seemed to hang in the air and its trajectory looked high. But then it dropped and I heard it hit either turkey or limb. The gobbler flushed straight back into the thick hammock. I dropped the bow and began busting through palmettos, briars, and mud. I reached the tree the gobbler had exploded from and raced another 50 yards in the direction of his flight. And then I began listening. If the bird was hit, I should hear him flopping in the palmettos or falling from a tree.

Five long minutes of dead silence passed. The thick hardwood and palm hammock about me grew darker and darker. And then I heard the crash of a turkey falling through limbs. I pinpointed the source of the noise as about 50 yards further into the hammock and 10° to my left. I raced to that point praying that the gobbler would flop one last time in the noisy palmettos. Now, it was almost black dark on the forest floor. Another few minutes of dead silence passed and I was almost ready to go back to the car for a flashlight. And then I heard a big wing slap palmettos almost under my feet—and suddenly I was on top of a mass of warm feathers, and a fine young gobbler which weighed twelve pounds even! The arrow had sliced almost halfway through the neck just above the point of aim.

Sure, luck played a big part in giving me this great moment in turkey hunting, and in giving me my other two gobblers with a bow. But the bowhunter must make his own luck—by spending long hours in the woods until it comes along, and by leaving no stone unturned in preparing for the hunt and in selecting the precise tackle and tactics most likely to give it to him. Studying the basic bowhunting tackle tips and the hunting tactics already detailed in preceding chapters should make any hunter 90% ready to bowhunt turkeys, for there is no essential difference in basic gun and bow hunting tactics in the spring or in the fall, and with or without a call. But to be *100%* ready for *bowhunting* turkeys, four additional factors of vital importance must be fully appreciated and considered on every hunt. Let's call them the finer points of turkey hunting with a bow.

THE FINER POINTS OF BOWHUNTING TURKEYS

The critical importance of *total* camouflage, of drawing at the *right* moment, of holding draw movements to a *minimum,* and the mandatory requirements for *pinpoint* accuracy: these are the four demanding factors which make successful bowhunting for turkeys difficult and different from gun hunting.

Complete camouflage is the cardinal rule wherever legal. Where red or orange is required, wear only a cap or vest.

The Importance of Total Camouflage

Only total camouflage of my bow, quiver, and every arrow, including fletchings, as well as camouflage of my clothing, face and hands, enabled me to remain undetected until I could make my draw on the first and second gobblers I bagged with the bow. (Approaching darkness shielded my draw on the third.) During both the first two successful draws using available brush for concealment also helped, but the brush alone would not have done the job. I *know* this from the many other times I have attempted to draw from a well concealed position, but without my bow or arrows being camouflaged. In *every* one of these cases, the gobbler detected me and spooked.

As previously stressed, a sharp-eyed gobbler can spot a poorly camouflaged hunter and take evasive action *ten times* faster than a hunter can spot a gobbler and even point a gun, much less raise a bow and draw. Unlike deer, turkeys are *not* color blind. And to shoot a turkey from even the best blind, the bowhunter must expose a part of himself and his bow. It is precisely for these important reasons that the bowhunter's camouflage must be *total* when he's hunting turkeys. Re-study Chapter 1 for tips on paints, tapes, face nets, and gloves required to accomplish this.

The Importance of Drawing At The Right Moment And With Minimum Movement

When bowhunting turkeys, the absolute necessity for making an undetected draw depends upon two other factors just as critical as total camouflage. The first is drawing at a *moment* when the turkey cannot possibly see you or when his attention and radar eyes are focused away from you. The second is keeping both your bow and body movement to an absolute minimum. Even if you and your tackle are completely camouflaged, attempting to draw at a moment when a turkey's attention and eyes are focused even in your general direction or considerable or fast movement of your body or bow, *no matter where* the bird's eyes and attention are focused, will likely guarantee your being detected and defeated. I know because of the many times I have been detected and defeated.

I drew on that first gobbler only when he walked behind that palmetto clump where he could not possibly see me; on the second only when his attention and eyes were focused directly away from me and on his buddy chasing the grasshopper; and on the third only when poor light shielded my draw.

Make your draw only when your quarry is within range and his head is behind a tree or bush, or looking the other way.

I shot the first turkey from the same crouched position on my knees I was forced to take when I spotted him so suddenly; and the second from the same comfortable standing position the well prepared blind enabled me to occupy throughout his approach. And in both cases, I had eased my bow in the direction of the expected shot long before the draw. Each of these important precautions enabled me to minimize both bow and body movement when that critical moment for the draw and release arrived. The gun hunter can sometimes make a mistake in these areas and still have a chance to swing his gun and bag his gobbler—but not the bowhunter. The turkey's reflexes are so fast that being detected, or even suspicioned, before or during the draw will end the bowhunter's game every time.

Of course, making the slightest noise as a turkey approaches can also focus his attention on your position and make a successful draw impossible. It was for this reason that Chapter 1 emphasized the importance of *noiseless* as well as camouflaged clothing. And it was for this same reason that I cleared every leaf and twig out of the floor of the blind from which I bagged my second gobbler. A worn slot in a quiver which might cause a spare arrow to rattle during the draw, or loose change or car keys or compass or knife in the pocket, are all potential noise sources which could cost you a gobbler. So, never carry an arrow in a worn quiver slot. And wrap your compass and knife in cloth or tissues. Hide your keys near the car and leave change in car or camp.

The Importance of Pinpoint Accuracy

The entire body of a turkey is smaller than the vital chest cavity of a deer. And an arrow will kill a turkey cleanly only if it penetrates his grapefruit-size upper body cavity or his long neck or head. This requires shooting with near pinpoint accuracy. No bowhunter should hunt turkeys until he is reasonably capable of such accuracy within a predetermined range—and he should not shoot at greater ranges unless the turkey's lower non-vital parts are protected by a limb, log, or other solid object which would stop a low flying arrow. A turkey hit in the lower body cavity or a leg will usually fly a great distance and never be retrieved.

Where Should The Bowhunter Aim?

High and forward is the important rule. Any high forward shot is likely to kill cleanly or miss completely. A low or rearward shot will either cripple or miss. It was for these reasons that I aimed high and forward on all three gobblers I bagged with a bow. Of course, I've also missed a few gobblers with slightly high and wide arrows by following this aiming rule. But more important, I have *never* crippled or lost one while adhering to it.

It's important to be very specific on this business of where to aim an arrow at a turkey, for most hunters have little chance to study the unique shape and unusual stance of a turkey before the moment for the draw arrives. Unlike deer and most big game, the turkey stands almost upright like a man, unless he is strutting or feeding. When he's facing generally sideways to the hunter, as was my first turkey with a bow, there are two good high and forward aiming points. If the turkey is in very close range and you're good enough, the exact center of his long neck is a good choice. Of course, a small error on either side of your aiming point will cause a clean miss; but if this to-the-side error is minute, your arrow can fly several inches *low* or *high* and you'll still get a neck or head hit and a clean kill. This is an attractive shot to consider since estimating exact range is the bowhunter's biggest problem; and for this reason arrow error is more likely to be high or low, rather than right or left.

The second good high and forward aiming point when a turkey is facing generally sideways to the hunter is the exact center of the turkey's *upper* body cavity, the point of aim I used on my first gobbler with a bow. This means aiming just above the center of the *upper* half of the turkey's body—*not* at the center of the *whole* body, or even at the center of its upper half. Remember that vital grapefruit-size *upper* body cavity lies closer to the turkey's back than to the bottom of its breast. If you aim at this point, your arrow can be two

This would be an ideal bow shot. The best aiming point would be at the juncture of the neck and body.

or three inches high—or low—or right—or left—of the aiming
point and you'll still get a sure kill.

When a turkey is facing generally *towards* you, as was
my second gobbler with a bow, or generally *away from you,*
as was my third, the best high and forward aiming point is
the *exact juncture of the neck and the body.* By aiming at this
point, the arrow can be as much as ten inches high or eight
inches low and you'll still penetrate the neck or upper body
cavity and get a clean kill. And if it flies up to eight inches low
and a couple of inches wide, it will still do the job cleanly. Of
course, if the arrow flies high and more than an inch to the
right or left, you'll miss cleanly. But this risk is a small price
to pay for the certain knowledge that your arrow would have
to fly nearly a foot low to only wound.

One final point on how *not* to shoot a turkey should be
emphasized. The bowhunter should never shoot at a gobbler
while he's strutting. While strutting, every feather on the bird
is erect and his head and neck are squeezed down into the
ruffed feathers. During this condition, an old tom looks like
a big round ball of feathers and picking a lethal aiming point
with precision is very difficult. One of the best times to *draw*
on an old tom, however, *is* when he's in full strut and facing
generally away from you, for his fanned tail shielding his low
contracted head will keep him from seeing you. However,
*release only when he drops the strut and is again standing in
an upright position.* If he holds the strut too long for you to
hold your draw, say "PUTT!" and he'll immediately whip
upright and stand motionless for a second. If you're at full
draw and ready to release, that should be all the time you
need.

Tips On Retrieving Bow-Hit Turkeys

Even when hit with a sharp broadhead in the vital neck
or upper body cavity, a turkey may flush and fly for 50 or 100
yards before falling, as did my first and third gobblers. Always mark very carefully the direction that a hit or possibly
hit turkey flies or runs. You may see him go down. If so,
mark that exact spot, and proceed to it immediately, never

Sharp arrows are as important in turkey hunting as in deer hunting.

taking your eyes off it. A dead turkey is mighty hard to spot visually on most forest floors.

If a hit turkey disappears while running or flying, head in the same direction with all possible speed. Then stop and *listen* when you're about 50 yards in from where you last saw him. If he's hit in a vital area, you'll probably hear him fall from a tree, as I did my third gobbler, or you'll probably hear him flopping somewhere on the ground. *Listening* is the only easy way to find a well-hit turkey that runs or flies off. And the only falling or flopping noises he makes might well occur within a very few minutes after being hit. So, *waste no time in getting to a promising spot to hear him.* If a turkey is poorly hit, you won't find him, regardless of what you do. And even if he's well hit, he won't leave a blood trail like a deer. So, you have nothing to lose by rushing to that promising listening position. Of course, if you hear nothing, your only option is to start cutting arcs in the direction the turkey was headed when you last saw him, and, at the same time, combing every inch of forest floor with your eyes.

These are the finer points of hunting gobblers with a bow that I've learned to respect over the years. Giving these factors serious consideration is the only means I know of for achieving any real probability for success in this toughest and most challenging of all shooting sports.

CHAPTER 17

What Will Turkey Hunting Be Like In The Year 2000?

What will turkey hunting be like in the year 2000? Will wild gobblers still gobble then? Some hunters doubt it. Will hunting pressure and evolution create a strain of "super" turkeys far more capable of outwitting hunters and of surviving wingbutt-to-elbow with man? Some hunters think so. Will fall turkey hunting be phased out and will severe controls be required on hunting seasons, bag limits, shells and guns? Many believe that these things, too, will come about. And the most critical question of all: Will we even have enough wild turkeys to hunt by 2000—and what must be done to increase the probability that we will?

Sound and factual answers to these questions are of interest or vital concern to every sportsman—for they shed cold light on the future of *all* wild game and *all* forms of hunting. To get such answers I went to six of the nation's leading turkey scholars. This commentary seeks to analyze and condense their thought provoking views in a clear- quick-look, and non-technical manner.

Five of the experts making this report possible are skilled wildlife biologists who have devoted their lives to the study of the wild turkey and its specific relationships to the hunter. Their collective reports and studies in these areas would fill many volumes, and they serve today as principal guidelines for wild turkey research and management across the nation. These distinguished biologists are: Professor Henry Mosby, Virginia Polytechnic Institute and State University; Mr. Wayne Bailey, North Carolina Wildlife Resources Commission; Mr. Vernon Bevill, South Carolina Wildlife and Marine Resources Commission; Mr. Lovett Williams, Florida Game and Freshwater Fish Commission; and Mr. Jerry Wuntz, Pennsylvania Game Commission. Our sixth expert is Mr. Tom Rodgers, capable and respected President of the National Wild Turkey Federation.

This commentary will first examine those questions and answers which are primarily stimulating and interesting to hunters. Then, it will treat those of an urgent and vital nature which concern the very survival of the wild turkey—and the great sport of hunting itself.

WILL GOBBLERS STILL BE GOBBLING BY THE YEAR 2000?

Thrilling to spine-tingling gobbling is the very essence of spring turkey hunting, the single big reason why most men pick up a gun and turkey call. Many feel certain that gobblers in their area are already gobbling with less frequency and gusto every year. And they are worried about this apparent trend eventually ending spring gobbler hunting as we know it today. Is this alleged trend real? Is it likely that a strain of turkeys is actually evolving which will gobble little or not at all? These are the first difficult questions which I posed to our panel of experts.

Wayne Bailey put the questions themselves into sharp and easy-to-see focus: "Theoretically, the gradual evolvement of strains of turkeys which rarely gobble *is* possible—through either consistent harvesting of birds that gobble best, or as a result of learned behavior, stemming from increased contact with hunters." *But are either of these possibilities likely to occur on a scale sufficient to seriously reduce future gobbling activity?* Wayne feels the answer is "NO," at least through the year 2000. "Since gobbling is spectacular, drawing the attention of all predators including man, it did not evolve, or sustain itself this long, without very good reason: namely to assure that mating occurs, even in areas with low turkey populations. Hence, gobbling has a strong species survival value perpetuated by genetic factors. I feel this value is unlikely to be significantly reduced by *any* factor by 2000."

Wayne also points out that most spring seasons are held *after* peak mating activity is over. Therefore, by the time most old dominant and talkative birds are harvested, they have already sired their young and contributed their genetic values to their offsprings. Lovett Williams and Vernon Bevill agree with Wayne, and add these pertinent thoughts: "The only way spring turkey hunting could effectively select against gobbling would be during a long period during which *virtually all talkative gobblers in an area were harvested.* This is extremely unlikely because old toms are so hard to bag, and because such intensive hunting pressure would also result in most non-gobbling toms being stumbled upon and taken as well. It is unlikely that such hunting pressure could occur, or that it would be tolerated by any game and fish agency. And, even if it did occur, it would not select against gobbling turkeys."

In spite of all these overwhelming reasons why gobblers *should* still be gobbling as well in 2000 as they do today, three of our six experts, like many hunters, are far from sure that they will be. Jerry Wuntz, Henry Mosby, and Tom Rodgers have studied a lot of turkeys over the years, and cite convincing evidence of already diminishing gobbling activity. From Pennsylvania, Wuntz reports "less gobbling activity in recent years, even though turkey populations remain high." Mosby reports that gobbling in his western Virginia area was "demonstrably less during the past four years." And Rodgers adds that gobblers in several areas he's recently studied "have tended to quiet down apparently because of increased hunting pressure." *Both Wuntz and Mosby believe that by 2000 we may*

Dedicated wildlife biologists are doing their best to stock trapped wild turkeys wherever habitat is available. The question: Will we sportsmen provide sufficient funds for the needed habitat?

well have strains of turkeys in some areas which rarely gobble. So, even the country's leading turkey scholars are divided on this difficult forecast. We can only hope that those are right who predict a continuation of that beautiful gobbler thunder which stirs the souls of so many of us—and which men of the future will need to hear more than ever.

WILL TURKEYS BE SUPER-WILD OR SUPER-TAME BY THE YEAR 2000?

History tells us that today's wary U.S. ruffed grouse was once as tame as a barnyard chicken. And observing the ruff's almost complete lack of fear of humans in wilderness areas of Canada today, convinces any hunter that this bit of history must be fact, not fiction. And we all know that whitetail deer have developed the cunningness to survive side-by-side with man in heavily populated farm and small woodlot situations. Will the same be true of the wild turkey by 2000? Or will he be contaminated and tamed by crossing with domestic turkeys?

Jerry Wuntz is an authority in this field. His paper *"Tolerances of Wild Turkeys to Human Disturbance and Limited Range,"* presented to the Northeastern Fish and Wildlife Conference in Portland in 1971, summarizes the most complete study ever completed in this specific area. It suggests that wild turkeys are *already* becoming sharp enough to survive and reproduce in small wooded units near urban areas, a fact which significantly broadens older concepts of large wilderness areas remote from man as required habitat. And Jerry adds: "Present day turkeys holding their own, as so many are in comparatively small and heavily hunted areas, have to be *sure enough* 'pure wild'. I believe that natural selection and hunting are going to reduce 'tameness' even further, and that the result will be even wilder and craftier turkeys by 2000—that is, if some dummies don't again start stocking a bunch of game-farm birds on top of them."

Lovett Williams jumped on the same point: "If you want a turkey that will nest in your azalias, let me recommend White Holland or Broadbreasted Bronze; but if you want a *sporting* bird, that can survive in the wild, instead of a pet, he's got to be really wild. Genetic contamination from domestic strains could be a problem, but fortunately, most half-breed turkeys cannot survive in the wilds long enough to reproduce. If full-blooded domestic and full-blooded wild turkeys cross and reproduce young, it is unlikely that the young would survive and contaminate the gene pool of the wild strain. On the other hand, should varieties be developed that are about ¾ to ⅞ wild, gene material from these semi-wild crosses could be introduced into and weaken wild strains. For this reason, I strongly oppose any effort to produce "suburban" wild turkey strains and support severe restrictions on the amount of wildness permitted in game farm turkeys. To sum it up, as long as we are faced only with the possibility of fully domestic turkeys crossing with fully wild turkeys, there is nothing serious to worry about in the future. I believe that in the past most strains of wild turkeys have remained relatively pure for this reason, and that this will continue to be the case."

Our other four experts essentially agree with Wuntz and Williams. All are convinced that our wild turkeys are going to be at least as wild, and probably even wilder, by the time 2000 rolls around—and that many will probably be crafty enough to survive wingbutt-to-elbow with man even in small woodlot situations.

WILL THE CHARACTER OF TURKEY HUNTING CHANGE BY 2000?

A rapid shift to "spring gobbler-only" seasons, more "bow-hunting-only" turkey hunting areas, tighter shell limits and controls over bag limits and numbers of hunters allowed into hunting areas—these are the principal changes our experts see in the character of turkey hunting by 2000. Fair allocations of hunting opportunity to an increasing number of hunters, they believe will require these changes.

Lovett Williams forecasts that as early as 1980 "most turkey hunting will be for spring gobblers only." Our other experts agree that this will probably be true at least by the year 2000, but for varying reasons. Tom Rodgers feels "our dyed-in-the-wool fall hunters are dying off and being replaced by "new-breed" spring hunters who like to get their turkey "the easy way." Vernon Bevill believes spring gobbler-only hunting will become increasingly necessary because numbers of hunters and turkeys harvested can be effectively controlled only during such hunts.

Wayne Bailey points out two other sound reasons for increased emphasis on spring gobbler-only hunting: "This type hunting gives the maximum number of hunters a rewarding recreational experience—and it cannot decrease the production of young turkeys." "However," he quickly adds: "I hope that we do not become emotionally trapped by spring-only concepts to the point where we cannot continue either-sex fall hunting where habitats and populations permit. Like quail and grouse, the wild turkey cannot be stockpiled. In areas of high turkey density and good habitat, we have proved that up to 30% of the females can be harvested without harm to the overall flock." Henry Mosby makes the same point: "In most areas where turkey populations are established and healthy we are currently sustaining unnecessary turkey losses to natural causes. Many of these could be harvested *by hunters* during fall hunts without affecting the average mortality rate of 60 to 70%."

The skyrocketing number of bowhunters in the U.S. (already more than 1.5 million) also will have heavy impact on future turkey hunting. More and more of these hunters are discovering that turkey hunting with a bow is the most challenging sport on the face of the earth. And, as Henry Mosby points out: "Opening more turkey areas to bowhunting-only is an excellent way to increase days of hunting with minimum impact on turkey populations. For this reason, it's bound to come about."

To fairly allocate available hunting opportunity and turkey resources, all our experts see controls as necessary and inevitable by the year 2000. As Mosby also points out, "Even if the number of turkey hunters does not increase drastically, the number of days each hunter will be able to hunt probably will." Because of these factors, they see necessary controls over the number of hunters allowed into most hunting areas at any one time, more permit-only hunts, one- or two-shell limit hunts, and much tighter bag limits. Lovett Williams even forecasts "lifetime limits here similar to those presently in effect for some species in Europe!"

Let's hope America's turkey hunting never comes to this. And let's do all we can to assure that it doesn't. Toward this end, I posed a last series of vital questions to our panel of experts. The answers to these questions explore the real heartbeat of future turkey hunting, and define the specific actions required to keep it strong. Some also have a direct bearing on the future of hunting itself.

HOW MANY WILD TURKEYS WILL THERE BE IN 2000?

Four of the experts interviewed fielded this question. Their estimates are projected in Chart 1, next.

CHART 1
U.S. Wild Turkey Population in Millions

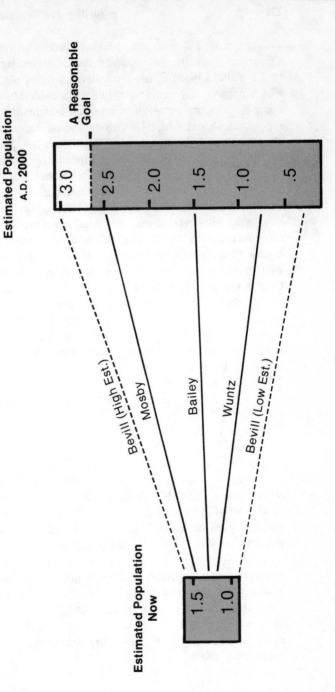

Estimated Population A.D. 2000

A Reasonable Goal

3.0
2.5
2.0
1.5
1.0
.5

Bevill (High Est.)
Mosby
Bailey
Wuntz
Bevill (Low Est.)

Estimated Population Now

1.5
1.0

As CHART 1 indicates, Mosby, Bailey, Wuntz, and Bevill agree that our current population level is on the order of 1 to 1.5 million birds. This level, several times higher than that which existed fifty years ago, reflects considerable credit upon our past and current wildlife research and management efforts supported almost entirely by dollars from hunters.

Parameters of population possibilities by the year 2000 are set by Vernon Bevill's high forecast of 3 million turkeys "if we do everything *right*"—but less than half a million "if we do everything *wrong*." He spells it out: "If current trends and rapid habitat loss continue, I expect the lower figure to be closer. However, if man starts taking more decisive actions *for* turkeys and other wildlife, and less *against* them, the higher figure could be closer." Mosby is optimistic that "we will probably increase the turkey's range and habitat" and forecasts 2.5 million birds by 2000. Wuntz is less optimistic and predicts less than one million. Bailey predicts "the nation-wide turkey population will probably peak at 1.5 to 2 million birds before the year 2000—and then decline, perhaps drastically, because of the human population boom and rapid loss of turkey habitat." A goal of 2.5 to 3 million turkeys by A.D. 2000, seen as possible by two of the four forecasters, appears to be a logical one for concerned conservationists to shoot for.

WHAT'S THE MOST IMPORTANT SINGLE REQUIREMENT FOR SAVING THE WILD TURKEY?

As Case 1 indicates, increasing and improving habitat faster than we are destroying it is the key requirement for more turkeys. As Case 2 illustrates, the converse could result in "endangered" population levels. All six turkey scholars interviewed agree on these central facts—and stress them beyond all others. Whether the American wild turkey flourishes—or dies out—or ultimately survives somewhere between these extremes—depends primarily upon what we do to its habitat. This is what Vernon Bevill meant when he pegged the future of the wild turkey on what man does *"for"*—and *"against"*—turkeys. Of course, providing more and better habitat to generate more turkeys will also depend upon other important supporting actions.

CHART 2

More and Better Habitat is the Key Factor

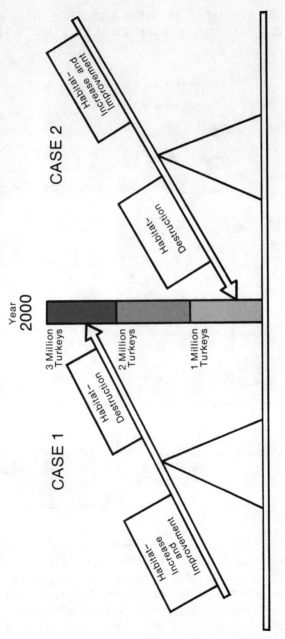

WHAT TOTAL ACTIONS ARE REQUIRED TO REACH A REASONABLE WILD TURKEY POPULATION GOAL?

CHART 3

Required Sequence of Actions

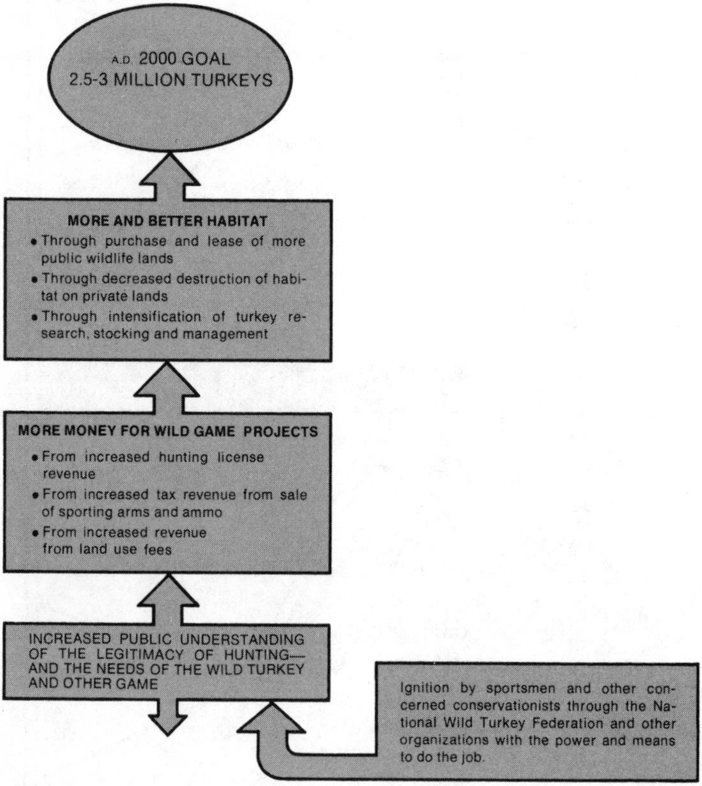

A.D. 2000 GOAL
2.5-3 MILLION TURKEYS

MORE AND BETTER HABITAT
- Through purchase and lease of more public wildlife lands
- Through decreased destruction of habitat on private lands
- Through intensification of turkey research, stocking and management

MORE MONEY FOR WILD GAME PROJECTS
- From increased hunting license revenue
- From increased tax revenue from sale of sporting arms and ammo
- From increased revenue from land use fees

INCREASED PUBLIC UNDERSTANDING OF THE LEGITIMACY OF HUNTING—AND THE NEEDS OF THE WILD TURKEY AND OTHER GAME

Ignition by sportsmen and other concerned conservationists through the National Wild Turkey Federation and other organizations with the power and means to do the job.

Chart 3 sums up the views of all six experts on the total sequence of actions required to achieve a reasonable wild turkey population goal. Note how the final goal, and every group of actions required to achieve it, depends upon supporting thrust actions. Every individual action listed must be executed effectively if we are to reach our goal—but not one can be executed with necessary effectiveness unless those which support it are also executed in the same manner. Let's now analyze each individual action required through the eyes of our experts.

HOW CAN WE INCREASE PUBLIC UNDERSTANDING OF THE LEGITIMACY OF HUNTING?

The future of hunting itself, as well as the required funding of all wildlife projects, requires *public support,* or at least tolerance. And, herein lies the first serious obstacle to preservation of the wild turkey and all other game as well.

Hunting faces a threatening and growing "image" problem which could become extremely acute by the turn of the century. Lovett Williams puts it bluntly: "Strong anti-hunting sentiment could well result in all hunting being outlawed in all or parts of some states by 2000." This problem stems primarily from the fact that an ever higher percentage of our young people are being born, raised, and educated in cities remote from hunting areas and opportunity. Many never come in close contact with anyone who understands the rewards of hunting or its essential contributions to wildlife. This problem is further accentuated by popular and well meaning Wild Kingdom—and Disney-type general media presentations, which quite properly mould a respect and love for wildlife—but which seldom get around to mentioning that most wild game habitat is generated by hunter respect and money. And, of course, half-true and misdirected anti-hunting stories and broadcasts also take their toll of young minds. No wonder, more and more young Americans, who have no compunction about eating beef, pork, lamb, or chicken, condemn the hunter who comes home with a more-humanely killed deer, turkey, or pheasant which his money alone produced. A recent survey published by Bear Archery indicates that the overwhelming majority of U.S. college students are already opposed to hunting. If we are to have adequate funds for wildlife, or even the chance to hunt by 2000, this is the tide which must be reversed.

"To turn the growing tide of public anti-hunting sentiment, it is the *true* image of hunting we must paint in the minds of young Americans—no made-up phony or half-true replica. If we tell it like it is, eventually we may be listened to and respected by most Americans, even by those who prefer not to hunt themselves." This is the concensus view of those dedicated experts who have devoted their lives to the mutually supporting needs of wildlife and the hunter.

They are telling us that we must get *facts* about hunting across to the public—facts about the hunter's vital contribution to all wildlife, as well as to the game he respects and hunts —facts about the esthetic values of hunting, and the true qualities of fair-chase, law-abiding sportsmanship which characterize the vast majority of hunters. We must also admit that we have "rotten apples" in our ranks, too, and do more to educate or purge them. And we must get such facts across, not only to those around us, but to vast segments of the American public as well.

We must also stop launching emotional attacks against "preservationists" and "anti-hunters," for they are among the most important people we need to tell our story to. If you expect people to listen, you don't hurl insults and criticisms at them. Instead, we must go to these people wih respect, reason, and facts—and with understanding that their *concern* for wildlife is as pure as our own. If wildlife is to survive at all, *all* conservationists, regardless of their views on hunting, must soon stop wasting their energies on fruitless family skirmishes related to the pros and cons of hunting, and join ranks to fight America's true enemies of wildlife. Speeding this day also must be a prime goal of our public information efforts.

Getting the true story of hunting across to the public also requires speaking with a single, organized, and effective voice through organizations with the power and means to make us heard across the nation. Several such organizations exist today—and every sportsman should belong to—and support them. You can order a complete list from The National Shooting Sports Foundation, Dept. SA, 1075 Post Road, Riverside, Conn. 06875. This same foundation is already doing an outstanding job in packaging key facts about hunting in the form of news releases, pamphlets, and films—and disseminating them to media representatives and important organizations of all kinds across the country. If you need an exciting and accurate background pamphlet or film about hunt-

Whether or not turkey hunters will enjoy moments like these in the year 2000 depends upon the actions you take today.

ing and its contribution to wildlife for your local television station, school, or civic club, write this foundation.

Lovett Williams also stresses the very important public educational responsibilities which state and federal game and fish agencies will have in the future. "The sport of hunting must be made more acceptable to the public. Fishing and hunting agencies must provide leadership in this area, rather than continuing to react ineffectively to anti-hunting sentiment."

There's no doubt that these agencies could be doing a much better job in this area than they are now. As one small but important example, they could post prominent and appropriate signs at the entrance of every sportsman-financed wildlife management area and wildlife refuge used for recreational purposes by the general public. "WELCOME!" should be the message. "YOUR ENJOYMENT OF THIS LAND AND THE WILDLIFE ON IT IS MADE POSSIBLE BY THE CONCERN AND LICENSE MONEY OF HUNTERS AND FISHERMEN." If such signs were posted nationwide, they would be read by millions of non-hunters including campers, picnickers, boaters and sightseers. And all would be reminded in a very real way of the sportsman's contribution to wildlife and the recreational needs of the general public.

Finally, every sportsman who wants to save the wild turkey should make it a special point to join the non-profit National Wild Turkey Federation, Dept. SA, P.O. Box 467, Edgefield, S.C. 29824. As its president Tom Rodgers points out, "Informing the public of the real needs of the wild turkey, including those related to hunting, is our primary objective. We need far more hunter support to do this important job the way it should be done."

Yes, the future of turkey hunting, as well as all other forms of hunting, and the essential funding of future wildlife projects, depends first of all upon increased public understanding of hunting as a legitimate sport. Every sportsman should do his part to see that this first vital task is accomplished. So should every federal and state wildlife conservation agency.

HOW CAN WE GENERATE MORE MONEY FOR WILD GAME PROJECTS?

It has always been the hunter who pays the big bills for our wild game projects, even though most benefit many species of non-hunted wildlife as well. This will continue to be the pattern, and rightly so. Therefore, it is vitally important that we convince those in our own ranks, as well as the general public, of the real needs of the wild turkey and other game. More money is one of those real needs. If we are to have more wild game to hunt by A.D. 2000, it's going to cost us more money to generate it. And we must be willing to pay the price. Four of the six experts interviewed stress this point. Vernon Bevill sums it up this way: "States must work to purchase or lease as much suitable turkey habitat as possible, and as *soon* as possible. This need alone is going to require mammoth amounts of money—and I don't believe it's too likely to get accomplished."

I'm a dedicated turkey hunter and Vernon's prediction offends me. If leaving a heritage of good hunting to those who follow me takes more money, I'm willing to pay my share of it. And I believe the overwhelming majority of American hunters will feel the same when they are convinced the need is there.

Needed additional funds for wild game projects must come from the same sources as in the past—primarily from increased revenue from hunting licenses, permits, and duck stamps—and from tax proceeds from the sale of sporting arms and ammunition. If the number of hunters continues to increase, so will the number of licenses and hunting arms sold. This will increase funds available for wild game projects. However, periodic increases, and probably high ones, in the cost of *individual* hunting licenses, permits and stamps will be required, too. There's little doubt about that: the cost of increasing wild game resources will indeed be monumental and just as subject to inflation as everything else.

Hunters also must be willing to pay more in lease, trespass, and other land-use fees for the privilege of hunting on private lands. We cannot reasonably expect the big timber and cattle companies, and other private landowners, to take those expensive actions necessary to raise more game unless benefitting hunters are willing to pay the bill. For example, profit from timber *and* wild game, not from timber alone, is the big incentive we must give those in the forest products industry. Without it, there's no way we can expect them to significantly modify profitable timbering operations to preserve essential wild game habitat.

HOW DO WE GET MORE AND BETTER TURKEY HABITAT?

The prereqisite requirements for more and better habitat are, of course, those we have just discussed: more money for wildlife and the public understanding and support required to generate it. But what must we buy with that money? The first answer is more public land suitable for the propagation of the wild turkey and other wildlife. This all experts interviewed agree upon with one set of words or another: "State game and fish agencies in particular must allocate more money for land acquisition," Wayne Bailey warns. In referring to the responsibilities of The National Wild Turkey Federation, as well as to state and federal wildlife agencies, Tom Rodgers stresses: "We must invest far more money in land acquisition, or use it to lease available habitat." The purchase and lease of as much public wildlife management land as possible, and as soon as possible, must, of course, be a goal of the highest priority, for everyone knows that lands suitable for this purpose are shrinking and growing more expensive with every year that passes.

The second important avenue to more and better turkey habitat is taking effective measures to decrease today's alarming destruction of wildlife habitat on private lands. As Vernon Bevill so aptly stresses: "Some of our best wild turkey populations today are on private lands. Thus, private landowners have a very great potential for helping the wild turkey." But instead of helping the turkey, many are now destroying vast areas of habitat with rapid and systematic precision. The problem stems primarily from the conversion of large wildlife areas of hardwoods, which turkeys and other wild game require to survive, to even-age short-rotation all-pine "plantations" which can support little wildlife of any kind. This problem is most acute in the southeastern states.

The Southeast Wild Turkey Sub-Committee of the National

Wild Turkey Federation recently resolved ". . . we do oppose the conversion of large areas to even-age short-rotation pine monoculture characterized by intensive site preparation accomplished by bulldozing, roll-chopping, and/or burning. We condemn these practices as destructive to wild turkey habitat and detrimental to many other wildlife species. All appropriate actions should be taken to terminate these practices and all landowners should be required to conform to present United States Forest Service forest management guidelines."

This resolution is commendable in that it publicly identifies a very real threat to our wild turkeys and other wildlife; however, identification of the threat alone will not erase it. We must develop reasonable, effective, and acceptable actions to accomplish this important goal. One of these has already been advanced: hunters *must* make the production of wild game, as well as timber and cattle, profitable on private lands by paying higher lease and trespass fees for the privilege of hunting. This and only this is likely to result in management of large and appropriate private areas for wildlife as well as wood and beef.

Another important avenue for increasing and improving turkey habitat on private lands is spelled out by Bevill: "By working closer with state and federal wildlife biologists, private landowners can increase and improve habitat for the wild turkey and other wildlife to a great degree without losing timber money. And game and fish agencies stand ready to stock suitable private lands with wild turkeys and other game at no cost to the landowner, and to help protect it from poaching—as long as legitimate hunters are allowed trespass on some reasonable basis. It is essential that we also stress this important message to landowners everywhere."

In order to accomplish the objectives just cited, and in order to generate the greatest possible number of turkeys and other wild game on available lands, far greater emphasis must also be placed on wildlife research. Bevill defines one vital part of this requirement, "Research must precisely identify the influences of man on the wild turkey's habitat and survival. It must produce more accurate data on rates of habitat losses and identify those responsible for them. Only then can all agencies, public and private, working with natural resources take really effective action to stop these losses."

Wayne Bailey adds: "Above all else, our research goals must be to learn more about turkey habitat needs, especially those regarding the importance of habitat diversity, clearings, and how clearings can best be managed for highest production of young." Jerry Wuntz agrees: "We must promote more effective research to find ways to enhance turkey populations on available lands. And we must put the results of that research into actual practice, an area we have been deficient in in the past."

Finally, Henry Mosby stresses that our wild turkey research must be vastly expanded in the areas of "turkey population dynamics and disease and parasite control, especially in high-density turkey areas." *All* these experts are shouting one single message: "We must greatly increase our wild turkey research efforts in order to stop habitat loss, to improve the habitat we have, and to generate the highest possible turkey populations on it."

In summation, to reach a reasonable wild turkey population goal by A.D. 2000, or even to save the wild turkey from extinction, we must take three vitally important steps: (1) we must increase public understanding of the legitimacy of hunting and the needs of the wild turkey; (2) we must generate more money for wildlife; and (3) we must provide more and better turkey habitat. This vital message comes from six experts who have devoted their lives to studying the wild turkey and its real needs. Its concepts apply to all wild game —and to all forms of hunting.

Appendix I

STATE AGENCIES TO CONTACT FOR HUNTING INFORMATION PLUS STATE-BY-STATE BREAKDOWN OF GOOD PUBLIC TURKEY HUNTING AREAS

STATE AGENCY TO CONTACT FOR HUNTING INFORMATION	GOOD PUBLIC TURKEY HUNTING AREAS
ALABAMA Dept. of Conservation and Natural Resources, Division of Game and Fish, 64 N. Union St., Montgomery 36104	*Managed Hunting Areas:* Barbour, Black Warrior, Blue Spring, Butler, Choccolocco, Coosa, Covington, Hollins, Lauderdale, Oakmulgee, Bob Boykin, Skyline, Thomas, Wolf Creek. *National Forests:* William B. Bankhead, Conecuh, Talladega, Tuskegee.

NOTE: Areas listed are those verified by the author or by state game and fish authorities as usually providing good turkey hunting. Some areas are not open for hunting every year. Contact state game and fish agencies listed for latest hunting regulations before planning hunts. Other good ones are listed in preceding chapters.

ARIZONA
Game and Fish Department, 2222 W. Greenway Road, Phoenix 85023

National Forests: Apache, Coconino, Coronado, Kaibab, Prescott, Sitgreaves, Tonto.

ARKANSAS
Game and Fish Commission, 2 Capitol Mall, Little Rock 72201

Managed Hunting Areas: Bull Shoals, White River.
National Forests: Ouachita, Ozark, St. Francis.

COLORADO
Division of Wildlife, 6060 N. Broadway, Denver 80216

Game Management Areas: Devil Creek, Escalante.
National Forests: Arapaho, Grand Mesa-Uncompahgre, Roosevelt, Routt, San Isabel, San Juan, White River.

FLORIDA
Game and Freshwater Fish Commission, 620 S. Meridian, Tallahassee 32304

Wildlife Management Areas: Apalachee, Aucilla, Blackwater, Fisheating Creek, Gulf Hammock, Lake Butler, Richloam, Steinhatchee, Tomoka.
National Forests: Apalachicola, Osceola.

GEORGIA
Dept. of Natural Resources, Trinity - Washington Bldg., 270 Washington St. S.W., Atlanta 30334

Public Hunting Areas: Chattahoochee, Clark Hill.
National Forests: Chattahoochee, Oconee.

IDAHO
Fish and Game Dept., 600 S. Walnut, Boise 83707

National Forest: Nezperce.

KENTUCKY
Dept. of Fish and Wildlife Resources, Capitol Plaza, Frankfort 40601

T.V.A. Area—Land Between the Lakes.

LOUISIANA
Wildlife and Fisheries Commission, 400 Royal St., New Orleans 70130

Game Management Areas: Chicago Mills.
National Forest: Kisatchie.

MARYLAND
Dept. of Natural Resources, Natural Resources Bldg., Rowe Blvd. and Taylor Ave., Annapolis 21401

Wildlife Management Areas: Dan's Mountain.
State Forests: Green Ridge, Potomac, Savage River, Swallow Falls.

MISSISSIPPI
Game and Fish Commission, Box 451, Jackson 39205

Wildlife Management Areas: Bienville, Chickasawhay, Choctaw, Dancing Rabbit, Homochitto, Leaf River, Red Creek, Sunflower, Tallahalla Creek, Wolf River.
National Forests: Bienville, Delta, Holly Springs, Homochitto, Tombigbee.

MISSOURI
Dept. of Conservation, North Ten Mile Dr., Jefferson City 65101

Wildlife Areas: Coldwater Tract, Gainesville, Mincy.
State Forests: Daniel Boone, Deer Run, Huzzah, Indian Trail, Meranec, Sam A. Baker.
National Forests: Clark, Mark Twain.

MONTANA
Dept. of Fish and Game, Helena 59601

National Forests: Custer, Lolo.

NEBRASKA
Game and Parks Commission, P.O. Box 30370, Lincoln 68503

Special Use Areas: Gilbert, Peterson.
National Forest: Nebraska.
National Grasslands: Oglala.

NEW MEXICO
Dept. of Game and Fish, State Capitol, Santa Fe 87801

Public Hunting Areas: Cimmaron Canyon, Terrero.
National Forests: Carson, Gila, Santa Fe, Cibola, Lincoln, Apache.

NEW YORK
Department of Environmental Conservation, Division of Fish and Wildlife, 50 Wolfe Road, Albany 12201

State Forest: Allegany.

NORTH CAROLINA
Wildlife Resources Commission, Albemarle Bldg., 325 N. Salisbury, Raleigh 27611

Game Lands: Casswell, Santeetlah, South Mountains, Standing Indian, Wayah Bald.
National Forest: Nantahala.

OKLAHOMA
Dept. of Wildlife Conservation, 1801 N. Lincoln, Box 53465, Oklahoma City 73105

Game Management Areas: Altus, Canton, Fort Supply.

PENNSYLVANIA
  Pennsylvania Game Commission, P.O. Box 1567, Harrisburg 17120

State Game Land Tracts: #74, #24, #31, #54, #29, #86, #26, #48, #73, #88, #12, #36, #141, #180, #13, #57, #210, #211, #80, #227, #14, #33, #100, #25, #44, #75, #30, #37.
National Forest: Allegheny.

SOUTH CAROLINA
  Wildlife and Marine Resources Dept., 1015 Main St., P.O. Box 167, Columbia 29202

National Forests: Sumter, Francis Marion.

SOUTH DAKOTA
  Dept. of Game, Fish and Parks, State Office Bldg., Pierre 57501

Public Shooting Areas: Battle Mountain, Beilage-Hepler, Buryanek.
National Forests: Black Hills, Custer.
National Glasslands: Oglala.

TENNESSEE
  Game and Fish Commission, P.O. Box 40747, Ellington Agricultural Center, Nashville 37220

T.V.A. Area—Land Between the Lakes.
National Forest: Cherokee.

TEXAS
  Parks and Wildlife Commission, John H. Reagan Bldg., Austin 78701

Wildlife Management Area: Gene Howe.

UTAH
  Division of Wildlife Resources, 1596 W. North Temple, Salt Lake City 84116

National Forests: Ashley, Dixie, Fishlake, Manti-Lasal.

VIRGINIA
  Commission of Game and Inland Fisheries, P.O. Box 11104, Richmond 23230

Wildlife Management Areas: Gathright, Highland County, Kerr Reservoir, Little North Mountain, Union-Bag Camp, A.P. Hill, Camp Pickett, Quantico.
State Forests: Appomatox-Buckingham, Cumberland, Prince Edward.
National Forests: George Washington, Jefferson.

WEST VIRGINIA
Dept. of Natural Resources, 1800 Washington St. East, Charleston 25305

Public Hunting Areas: Bluestone, Chief Cornstalk, Lewis Wetzel, Nathaniel Mountain, Short Mountain, Sleepy Creek.
National Forests: George Washington, Monongahela.

WYOMING
Game and Fish Commission, Box 1589, Cheyenne 82001

National Forest: Black Hills.

Index